I0007997

ARDUINO BEST DIY
10 PROJECTS

CONTENTS

ACKNOWLEDGMENTS

The writer might want to recognize the diligent work of the article group in assembling this book. He might likewise want to recognize the diligent work of the Raspberry Pi Foundation and the Arduino bunch for assembling items and networks that help to make the Internet Of Things increasingly open to the overall population. Yahoo for the democratization of innovation!

INTRODUCTION

The Internet of Things (IOT) is a perplexing idea comprised of numerous PCs and numerous correspondence ways. Some IOT gadgets are associated with the Internet and some are most certainly not. Some IOT gadgets structure swarms that convey among themselves. Some are intended for a solitary reason, while some are increasingly universally useful PCs. This book is intended to demonstrate to you the IOT from the back to front. By structure IOT gadgets, the per user will comprehend the essential ideas and will almost certainly develop utilizing the rudiments to make his or her very own IOT applications. These included ventures will tell the per user the best way to assemble their very own IOT ventures and to develop the models appeared. The significance of Computer Security in IOT gadgets is additionally talked about and different systems for protecting the IOT from unapproved clients or programmers. The most significant takeaway from this book is in structure the tasks yourself.

1.ARDUINO WHISTLE DETECTOR SWITCH USING SOUND SENSOR

As a child I was intrigued by a toy music vehicle which gets activated when you applaud, and after that as I grew up I thought about whether we can utilize the equivalent to flip lights and fans in our home. It is cool to simply turn on my Fans and lights by simply applauding as opposed to strolling my apathetic self to the switch board. Be that as it may, as a rule it would breakdown as this circuit will react to any noisy clamor in the earth, similar to a boisterous radio or for my neighbor's garden trimmer. Inspite the fact that building an applaud switch is likewise a fun undertaking to do.

It was at that point, when I ran over this Whistle Detecting strategy in which the circuit will distinguish for whistle. A whistle dissimilar to different sounds will have a uniform recurrence for a specific span and consequently can be recognized from discourse or music. So in this instructional exercise we will figure out how to identify whistle sound by interfacing Sound Sensor with Arduino and when a whistle is recognized we will flip an AC light through a transfer. En route we will likewise figure out how stable sign are gotten by mouthpiece and how to gauge recurrence utilizing Arduino. Sounds intriguing right so how about we begin with Arduino based Home Automation Project.

Materials Required

1. Sound Sensor Module
2. Arduino UNO
3. AC Lamp
4. Relay Module
5. Connecting Wires
6. Breadboard

Sound Sensor Working

Before we jump into the equipment association and code for this Home Automation Project, we should investigate the sound sensor. The sound sensor utilized in this module is demonstrated as follows. The working guideline of most stable sensors accessible in the market is like this, in spite of the fact that the appearance may change a piece.

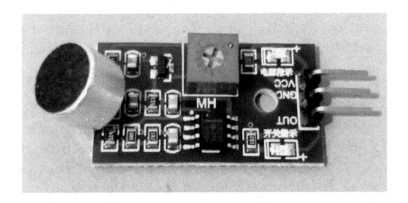

We probably aware the crude part in a sound sensor is the receiver. An amplifier is sort of transducer which converters sound waves (acoustical vitality) into electrical vitality. Fundamentally stomach inside the mouthpiece vibrates to the sound waves in the environment which produces electrical sign on its yield stick. However, these sign will be of extremely low greatness (mV) and henceforth can't be handled legitimately by a microcontroller like Arduino. Additionally as a matter of course stable sign are simple in nature consequently the yield from the receiver will be a sine wave with variable recurrence, however microcontrollers are computerized gadgets and subsequently work better with square wave.

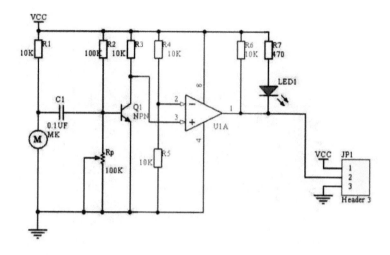

To enhance these low signal sine waves and convert them into square waves the module utilizes the on-board LM393 Comparator module as appeared previously. The low voltage sound yield from the mouthpiece is provided to one stick of the comparator through a speaker transistor while a reference voltage is determined to the next stick utilizing a voltage divider circuit including a potentiometer. At the point when the sound yield voltage from mouthpiece surpasses the preset voltage the comparator goes high with 5V (working voltage), else the comparator remains low at 0V. Along these lines low signal sine wave can be converter to high voltage (5V) square wave. The oscilloscope preview underneath demonstrates a similar where the yellow wave is the low signal sine wave and the blue on is the yield square wave. The affectability can be constrained by shifting the potentiometer on the module.

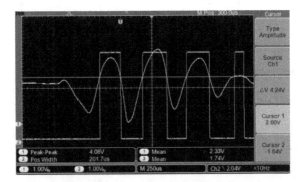

Measuring Audio Frequency on Oscilloscope

This sound sensor module will change over the sound waves in the air into square waves who's recurrence will be equivalent to the recurrence of the sound waves. So by estimating the recurrence of the square wave we can discover the recurrence of the sound flag in the environment. To ensure things are filling in as they are assumed I associated the sound sensor to my degree to test its yield signal.

I turned on the estimation mode on my degree to gauge the recurrence and utilized an Android application (Frequency Sound Generator) from the Play Store to produce sound sign of known recurrence. As should be obvious in the above GID the extension had the option to quantify sound sign with an entirely good precision, the estimation of recurrence showed in the degree is extremely near one shown on my telephone. Presently, that we realize the module is working lets continue with interfacing Sound sensor with Arduino.

Whistle Detector Arduino Circuit Diagram

The total circuit chart for the Arduino Whistle Detector Switch circuit utilizing Sound Sensor is appear underneath. The circuit was drawn utilizing Fritzing programming.

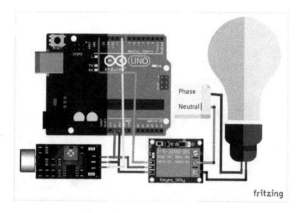

The Sound sensor and the Relay module is controlled by the 5V stick of the Arduino. The yield stick of the Sound sensor is associated with the advanced stick 8 of the Arduino, this is a result of the clock property of that stick and we will talk about progressively about this in the programming segment. The Relay module is activated by stick 13 which is additionally associated with the in-constructed LED on the UNO board.

On the AC supply side the impartial wire is straight-forwardly associated with the Common(C) stick of the Relay module while the Phase is associated with the Normally Open(NO) stick of the hand-off through the AC load (light). Along these lines when the hand-off is set off the NO stick will be associated with C stick and in this manner the light will gleam. Else the blub will stay killed. When the associations are made, my equipment looked somewhat like this.

Warning:

Working with AC circuit could get risky, be careful while taking care of live wires and maintain a strategic distance from shortcircuits. An electrical switch or grown-up supervision is suggested for individuals who are not experienced with gadgets. You have been cautioned!!

Measuring Frequency with Arduino

Like our degree perusing the recurrence of the approaching square waves, we need to program out Arduino to compute recurrence. We have as of now figured out how to do this in our Frequency Counter instructional exercise utilizing the beat in capacity. Yet, in this instructional exercise we will utilize the Freqmeasure library to gauge recurrence to get exact outcomes. This library utilizes the inside clock hinder on stick 8 to quantify to what extent a heartbeat remains ON. When the time is measure we can ascertain the recurrence utilizing the formulae F=1/T. Anyway since we are utilizing the library straightforwardly we need not dive into the register subtleties and math of how recurrence is estimated. Library can be downloaded from the connection beneath:

- Recurrence Measure Library by pjrc

The above connection will download a compress record, you would then be able to add this compress document to your Arduino IDE by following the way Sketch - > Include Library - > Add .ZIP Library.

Note: Using the library will debilitate the analog-Write usefulness on stick 9 and 10 on UNO since the clock will be involved by this library. Likewise these pins will change if different sheets are utilized.

Programming your Arduino for detecting Whistle

In this heading I will clarify the program by breaking it into little bits.

Like consistently we start the program by including the required libraries and pronouncing the required factors. Ensure you have included the FreqMeasure.h library as of now as clarified in above heading. The variable state speaks to the condition of the LED and the factors recurrence and progression is utilized to yield the deliberate recurrence and its congruity separately.

```
#include <FreqMeasure.h>//https://github.com/
PaulStoffregen/FreqMeasure

double sum=0;

int count=0;

bool state = false;

int frequency;

int continuity =0;
```

Inside the void arrangement work, we start the sequential screen at 9600 baud rate for investigating. At that point utilize the FreqMeasure.begin() capacity to introduce the stick 8 for estimating the recurrence. We additionally proclaim that stick 13 (LED_ BUILTIN) is yield.

```
void setup() {

  Serial.begin(9600);

  FreqMeasure.begin(); //Measures on pin 8 by default

  pinMode(LED_BUILTIN, OUTPUT);

}
```

Inside the limitless circle, we continue tuning in on stick 8 utilizing the capacity FreqMeasure.available(). In case there is an approaching sign we measure the recurrence utilizing the FreqMeasure.read(). To avoid mistake because of clamor we measure 100 examples and taken a normal of that. The code to do the equivalent is demonstrated as follows.

```
if (FreqMeasure.available()) {

  // average several reading together
```

```
sum = sum + FreqMeasure.read();

count = count + 1;

if (count > 100) {

  frequency = FreqMeasure.countToFrequency(
sum / count);

  Serial.println(frequency);

  sum = 0;

  count = 0;

}

}
```

You can utilize the Serial.println() work here to check the estimation of the recurrence for your whistle. For my situation the worth got was from 1800Hz to 2000Hz. The whistle recurrence of the vast majority will fall in this specific range. Be that as it may, even different seems like music or voice may fall under this recurrence so to recognize them we will screen for congruity. In the event that the recurrence is consistent for multiple times, at that point we affirm it to be a whistle sound. Along these lines, in the event that the recurrence is between 1800 to 2000, at that point we increase the variable called congruity.

```
if (frequency>1800 && frequency<2000)

{ continuity++; Serial.print("Continuity -> ");
Serial.println(continuity); frequency=0;}
```

On the off chance that the estimation of progression comes to or surpasses three, at that point we change the condition of the LED by flipping the variable called state. In the event that the state is as of now evident we change it to false and tight clamp versa.

```
if (continuity >=3 && state==false)

{state = true; continuity=0; Serial.printl-
n("Light Turned ON"); delay(1000);}

if (continuity >=3 && state==true)

{state = false; continuity=0; Serial.printl-
n("Light Turned OFF"); delay(1000);}
```

Arduino Whistle Detector Working

When the code and the equipment are prepared we can begin testing it. Ensure the associations are right and catalyst the module. Open the sequential screen and begin whistling, you can see the estimation of coherence being augmented lastly killing on or the Lamp. An example preview of my sequential screen is demonstrated as follows.

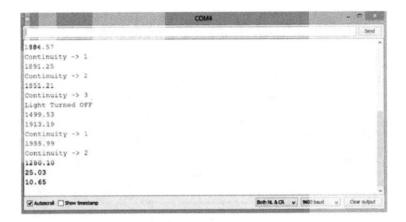

At the point when the sequential screen says Light turned on the stick 13 will be made high and the hand-off will be trigged to turn on the Lamp. Additionally the light will be killed when the sequential screen says Light killed. When you have tried the working you can control the set-up utilizing a 12V connector and begin controlling your AC Home Appliance utilizing whistle.

Expectation you comprehended the instructional exercise and appreciated discovering some new information.In case you have any issue in getting things work, leave them in the remark area or utilize our gathering for other specialized quires.

Code

```
/*Arduino Whitsle Detector Switch Program
 * Detects the whistles from pin 8 and toggles pin 13


#include     <FreqMeasure.h>//https://github.com/
PaulStoffregen/FreqMeasure
void setup() {
 Serial.begin(9600);
```

```
 FreqMeasure.begin(); //Measures on pin 8 by default
 pinMode(LED_BUILTIN, OUTPUT);
}
double sum=0;
int count=0;
bool state = false;
float frequency;
int continuity =0;
void loop() {
 if(FreqMeasure.available()) {
  // average several reading together
  sum = sum + FreqMeasure.read();
  count = count + 1;
  if(count > 100) {
   frequency = FreqMeasure.countToFrequency(sum /
count);
   Serial.println(frequency);
   sum = 0;
   count = 0;
  }
 }

   if(frequency>1800 && frequency<2000)
   { continuity++; Serial.print("Continuity -> "); Ser-
ial.println(continuity); frequency=0;}

   if(continuity >=3 && state==false)
    {state = true; continuity=0; Serial.println("Light
Turned ON"); delay(1000);}

   if(continuity >=3 && state==true)
    {state = false; continuity=0; Serial.println("Light
Turned OFF"); delay(1000);}
```

```
    digitalWrite(LED_BUILTIN, state);
}
```

◆ ◆ ◆

2.HOW TO USE BH1750 AMBIENT LIGHT SENSOR WITH ARDUINO

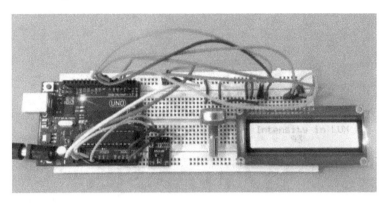

W hen you take your telephone in daylight or in high lighting, at that point it consequently modifies the brilliance as per the lighting conditions. The greater part of the presentation gadgets now a days, regardless of whether it's a TV or cell phone, have the Ambient Light Sensor inside to alter the splendor consequently. Today in this instructional exercise, we will utilize one such sensor BH1750 Light Sensor Module and interface it with Arduino and demonstrate the Lux esteem over 16x2 LCD.

Introduction to BH1750 Digital Light Sensor Module

The yield of this sensor is in LUX (lx), so it doesn't require any further estimations. Lux is the unit to gauge Light power. It quantifies the force as indicated by the measure of light hitting on a specific region. One lux is equivalent to one lumen for each square meter.

The sensor works on voltages from 2.4V to 3.6V (normally 3.0V) as well as it expends current of 0.12mA. This sensor has a wide range and high goals (1-65535lx) and moreover, the estimation variety is additionally little (about +/ - 20%). It can likewise work freely with no outside part.

Albeit a LDR sensor can be utilized to control the gadgets dependent on lighting conditions yet it isn't so exact. We have utilized LDR sensor to assemble many light controlled applications:

1. Arduino Light Sensor Circuit utilizing LDR

2. Dim Detector utilizing LDR and 555 Timer IC

3. Basic LDR Circuit to Detect Light

4. Arduino Color Mixing Lamp utilizing RGB LED as well as LDR

Arduino BH1750 Ambient Light Sensor **Circuit Diagram**

The circuit graph to interface BH1750 Light sensor with Arduino is demonstrated as follows.

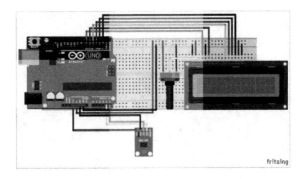

I2C correspondence pins SDA and SCL of BH1750 are associated with Arduino stick A4 and A5 separately for I2C correspondence. As we probably am aware the working voltage for the sensor is 3.3v so VCC and GND of BH1750 are associated with 3.3V and GND of Arduino. For LCD, information pins (D4-D7) are associated with computerized pins D2-D5 of Arduino and RS and EN pins are associated with D6 and D7 of Arduino. V0 of LCD is associated with pot and a 10k pot is utilized to control the splendor of LCD.

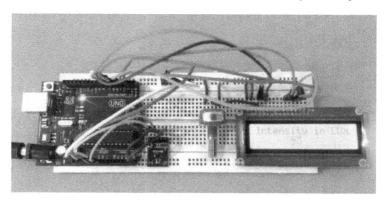

Programming Arduino for interfacing BH1750 Light Sensor

The programming segment for utilizing this LUX sensor with Arduino is extremely simple. In case there is a library accessible for this sensor, yet we can likewise utilize it without that.

Right off the bat, we've included header documents for LCD and I2C convention.

```
#include<Wire.h>

#include<LiquidCrystal.h>
```

In arrangement work, we've introduced both LCD and sensor and printed the opening message on LCD.

```
void setup()
```

```
{

  Wire.begin();

  lcd.begin(16,2);

  lcd.print(" BH1750 Light ");

  lcd.setCursor(0,1);

  lcd.print("Intensity Sensor");

  delay(2000);

}
```

Here BH1750_Read and BH1750_Init capacities are utilized to peruse and compose the Lux esteems individually. The Wire.beginTransmission() work is utilized to start the transmission and Wire.request-From(address, 2) work is utilized to peruse registers where 2 demonstrates the quantity of registers.

Further Wire.endTransmission() is utilized to part of the arrangement Wire.write() work is utilized to go to the ideal register by entering the location of that register in it.

```
int BH1750_Read(int address)
```

```
{

  int i=0;

  Wire.beginTransmission(address);

  Wire.requestFrom(address, 2);

  while(Wire.available())

  {

    buff[i] = Wire.read();

    i++;

  }

  Wire.endTransmission();

  return i;

}

void BH1750_Init(int address)

{

  Wire.beginTransmission(address);
```

```
Wire.write(0x10);

Wire.endTransmission();

}
```

In circle work, we are printing the ongoing lux esteems over LCD. First look at the arrival esteem from BH1750_Read work with 2, and afterward begin printing the Lux esteems in the event that it is equivalent to 2. Here the qualities are contrasted and 2 in light of the fact that BH1750_Read capacity restores the estimation of register check and we are perusing just 2 registers. So when it spans to 2, the program begins printing the LUX estimations of light power.

At that point an equation is utilized to get the qualities from both the registers and gap them by 1.2, which is the estimation exactness.

```
void loop()

{

  int i;

  uint16_t value=0;
```

```
BH1750_Init(BH1750address);

delay(200);

if(2==BH1750_Read(BH1750address))

{

  value=((buff[0]<<8)|buff[1])/1.2;

  lcd.clear();

  lcd.print("Intensity in LUX");

  lcd.setCursor(6,1);

  lcd.print(value);

}

  delay(150);

}
```

At long last catalyst the Arduino and transfer the program into Arduino. When program is transferred the LCD begins demonstrating the light power in LUX units. You can likewise fluctuate the qualities by changing the light force around the sensor.

Anbazhagan k

Code

```
#include<Wire.h>
#include<LiquidCrystal.h>


int BH1750address = 0x23;
byte buff[2];
LiquidCrystal lcd (7,6,5,4,3,2); //RS, E, D4, D5, D6, D7
void setup()
{
 Wire.begin();
 //Serial.begin(9600);
 lcd.begin(16,2);
 lcd.print(" BH1750 Light ");
 lcd.setCursor(0,1);
 lcd.print("Intensity Sensor");
 delay(2000);
}


void loop()
{
 int i;
 uint16_t value=0;
 BH1750_Init(BH1750address);
 delay(200);

  if(2==BH1750_Read(BH1750address))
  {
```

```
value=((buff[0]<<8)|buff[1])/1.2;
lcd.clear();
lcd.print("Intensity in LUX");
lcd.setCursor(6,1);
lcd.print(value);


 //Serial.print(val);
//Serial.println("[lux]");
}
delay(150);
}


int BH1750_Read(int address)
{
int i=0;
Wire.beginTransmission(address);
Wire.requestFrom(address, 2);
while(Wire.available())
{
 buff[i] = Wire.read();
 i++;
}
Wire.endTransmission();
return i;
}


void BH1750_Init(int address)
{
```

```
Wire.beginTransmission(address);
Wire.write(0x10);
Wire.endTransmission();
}
```

3.RS-485 MODBUS SERIAL COMMUNICATION WITH ARDUINO AS MASTER

I n the past instructional exercise we found out about Modbus RS-485 Serial Communication with Arduino as Slave.Arduino will be utilized MODBUS Master and speak with MODBUS slave. Here MODBUS Slave Software introduced PC will be utilized as MODBUS Master. In this way, how about we start by a short presentation about the RS-485 and Modbus.

RS-485 Serial Communication

RS-485 is a nonconcurrent sequential correspondence convention which doesn't not require clock. It utilizes a system called differential sign to move paired information starting with one gadget then onto the next. It gives a Half-Duplex correspondence when utilizing two wires and Full-Duplex requires 4 fours wires.

Connecting RS-485 with Arduino

RS-485 Module can be associated with any microcontroller having sequential port. For utilizing RS-485 module with microcontrollers, a module called 5V MAX485 TTL to RS485 which depends on Maxim MAX485 IC is required as it permits sequential correspondence over long separation of 1200 meters. It is bidirectional and half duplex and has information move pace of 2.5 Mbps. This module requires a voltage of 5V.

Pin-Out of RS-485:

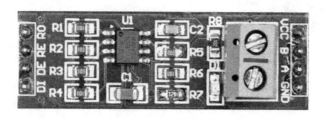

Pin Name	Use
VCC	5V

A	Non-inverting Receiver Input Non-Inverting Driver Output
B	Inverting Receiver Input Inverting Driver Output
GND	GND (0V)
RO	Receiver Out (RX pin)
RE	Receiver Output (LOW-Enable)
DE	Driver Output (HIGH-Enable)
DI	Driver Input (TX pin)

USB to RS-485 Converter Module:

This is a USB to RS485 Converter Adapter module which supports WIN7, XP, Vista, Linux, Mac OS and gives a simple to utilize RS485 interface by methods for utilizing COM port in the PC. This module is fitting and-play gadget. There are no direction structures, whatever is sent to the Virtual COM Port is naturally changed over to RS485 and the other way around. The module is totally self-controlled from the USB transport. Along these lines, no need of outer power supply for activity.

It appears as a Serial/COM port as well as is available from applications or hyper-terminal. This converter gives half-duplex RS-485 correspondence. The Baud rate range is 75 bps to 115200 bps, most extreme up to 6 Mbps.

To utilize this gadget there are different Modbus Software accessible in the web. In this instructional exercise programming called Modbus Slave programming from Witte Software is utilized. The product can be downloaded from the site www.modbustools.com.

Modbus Slave Software

Modbus Slave application gets values from any Modbus Master gadget by utilizing sequential correspondence port. It is an information correspondence test programming. Prior to utilizing the product, following things must be known. For more data, allude programming manual.

Slave ID:

Each slave in a system is doled out an exceptional unit address from 1 to 127. At the point when the ace solicitations information, the primary byte it sends is the Slave address. Along these lines each slave knows after the primary byte whether to overlook the message.

Modbus Registers:

Discrete Output Coils:

It is a 1-piece register and they are utilized to control discrete yields and can be perused or composed. They have register numbers from (1 to 9999).

Discrete Input:
It is a 1-piece register and utilized as data sources and must be perused. They have register numbers from (10001 to 19999).

Input Register:

It is a 16-piece register utilized for info and must be perused. They have register numbers from (30001 to 39999).

Holding Register:

It is a 16-piece register and can be perused or composed. They have register numbers from (40001 to 49999).

Modbus Function codes:

Function Code	Action	Table Name
04 (04 hex)	Read	Analog Input Registers
03 (03 hex)	Read	Analog Output Holding Registers
06 (06 hex)	Write single	Analog Output Holding Register
16 (10 hex)	Write multiple	Analog Output Holding Registers

Supported Coil Function codes:

Function Code	Action	Table Name
02 (02 hex)	Read	Discrete Input Contacts
01 (01 hex)	Read	Discrete Output Coils
05 (05 hex)	Write single	Discrete Output Coil
15 (0F hex)	Write multiple	Discrete Output Coils

CRC:

CRC represents Cyclic Redundancy check. It is two

bytes added to the part of the arrangement message for mistake location.

Components Required

Hardware

1. USB to RS-485 Converter Module
2. Arduino UNO
3. MAX-485 TTL to RS-485 Converter Module
4. Push Buttons (2)
5. 10k-Resistor (2)
6. 16x2 LCD display
7. 10k Potentiometer

Software

- **Modbus Slave**

Circuit Diagram

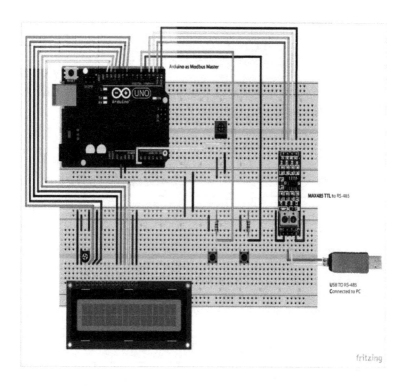

Circuit Connections between MAX-485 TTL to RS-485 converter module and Arduino UNO:

Arduino UNO	MAX-485 TTL to RS-485 Converter Module
0(RX)	RO
1(TX)	DI
3	DE
2	RE

+5 V	VCC
GND	GND

Circuit Connections between MAX-485 TTL to RS-485 Module and USB to RS-485 converter:

MAX-485 TTL to RS-485 Converter Module	USB to RS-485 Module Connected with PC
A	A
B	B

Circuit Connections between Arduino UNO and 16x2 LCD display:

16x2 LCD	Arduino UNO
VSS	GND
VDD	+5 V
V0	To potentiometer centre pin for contrast control of LCD
RS	8
RW	GND
E	9
D4	10
D5	11
D6	12

D7	13
A	+5V
K	GND

Two Push Buttons with Pull down resistor of 10k are likewise associated with the Arduino Pins 4 and 5. A 10K potentiometer is utilized to give Analog information incentive to the Arduino stick A0.

After the circuit associations the total arrangement resembles this.

Programming Arduino Uno as MODBUS Master

In this instructional exercise the Arduino Uno is designed as Modbus Master by utilizing Master Modbus Arduino coding with the assistance of Modbus Master library. Here Arduino Uno has two drive catches and a potentiometer to send the qualities from Modbus Master Arduino to Modbus Slave programming.

For utilizing Modbus in Arduino UNO, a library <ModbusMaster.h> have been utilized. This library is utilized for speaking with RS-485 Modbus Master or Slave through RTU convention. Download the Modbus Master as well as include the library in the sketch by following Sketch->include library->Add .zip Library.

Complete code is given toward the end. Here we have clarified has some significant strides underneath.

To start with, incorporate the ModbusMaster and Liquid Crystal Library:

```
#include <ModbusMaster.h>

#include <LiquidCrystal.h>
```

Next characterize the Pin names that are associated between the MAX485 TTL to RS-485 converter module and Arduino UNO.

```
#define MAX485_DE   3
```

#define MAX485_RE_NEG 2

Instate hub object for class ModbusMaster.

ModbusMaster node;

At that point compose two capacities preTrasnmission() and postTrasmission() for making the Pins RE and DE of Max485 TTL to RS-485 convertor module high or low to Transmit or Receive information.

```
void preTransmission()

{

  digitalWrite(MAX485_RE_NEG, 1);

  digitalWrite(MAX485_DE, 1);

}

void postTransmission()

{

  digitalWrite(MAX485_RE_NEG, 0);

  digitalWrite(MAX485_DE, 0);
```

```
}
```

Next in the void arrangement (), the LCD is set in 16x2 mode and an appreciated message is shown and cleared.

```
lcd.begin(16,2);

  lcd.print("Hellow_world");

  delay(3000);

  lcd.clear();

  lcd.print("Arduino");

  lcd.setCursor(0,1);

  lcd.print("Modbus Master");

  delay(3000);

  lcd.clear();
```

At that point RE and DE pins are set as OUTPUT pins and the pins 4 and 5 are set as INPUT pins (Push Buttons).

```
pinMode(MAX485_RE_NEG, OUTPUT);

pinMode(MAX485_DE, OUTPUT);

pinMode(4,INPUT);

pinMode(5,INPUT);
```

At first the DE as ell as RE pins of the MAX-485 TTL to RS-485 Converter Module is set LOW

```
digitalWrite(MAX485_RE_NEG, 0);

digitalWrite(MAX485_DE, 0);
```

Set the baud rate at 115200 as well as educate the Modbus Master with the slave ID 1.

```
Serial.begin(115200);

node.begin(1, Serial);
```

After that get back to proclamations are utilized so the RS-485 Transceiver is arranged appropriately.

```
node.preTransmission(preTransmission);

node.postTransmission(postTransmission);
```

Presently in the void circle()

- First the Analog worth is perused from the stick A0 that is associated with potentiometer.

```
float value = analogRead(A0);
```

- At that point ADC estimation of (0 to 1023) is kept in touch with the 0x40000 register for sending it to Modbus Slave by utilizing the accompanying articulation.

```
node.writeSingleRegister(0x40000,value);
```

- At that point the worth is additionally shown in the 16x2 LCD show

```
lcd.setCursor(0,0);

lcd.print("POT Val :");
```

```
lcd.print(value);
```

- Next the condition of the two-push catches is perused.

```
int a= digitalRead(4);

int b= digitalRead(5);
```

- What's more, contingent on the condition of the push catch, the worth 0x40001 for catch 1 and 0x40002 for catch 2 is kept in touch with the Modbus Slave and furthermore showed on LCD show.

```
if (a == 1)

{

  node.writeSingleRegister(0x40001,1);

  lcd.setCursor(0,1);

  lcd.print("S1: 1");

}

Else
```

```
{

  node.writeSingleRegister(0x40001,0);

  lcd.setCursor(0,1);

  lcd.print("S1: 0");

}

if (b == 1)

{

  node.writeSingleRegister(0x40002,1);

  lcd.setCursor(8,1);

  lcd.print("S2: 1");

}

else

{

  node.writeSingleRegister(0x40002,0);

  lcd.setCursor(8,1);
```

```
lcd.print("S2: 0");

}
```

Testing the Arduino UNO as RS485 MODBUS Master

After the circuit associations are finished and the code is transferred to Arduino Uno now its opportunity to interface the USB to RS-485 Module to the PC where the Modbus Slave Software is introduced.

Note: Open the gadget director and check the COM port as indicated by your PC where the USB to RS-485 Module is associated and afterward open the Modbus Slave programming.

1.The Modbus Slave Tool shows up as beneath and it demonstrates No Connection.

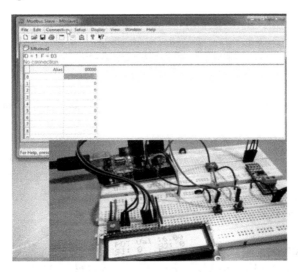

2. Next Open Connection->Connect and it shows up as beneath.

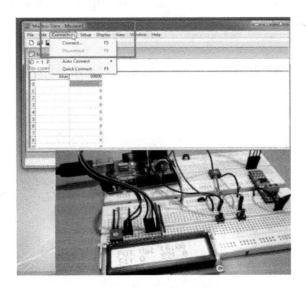

3. It demonstrates the beneath discourse box as this product is a preliminary form so click on Register Later

4. This preliminary programming pursues for 10 minutes opening it.

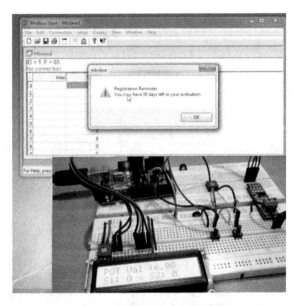

5. The association subtleties are demonstrated as follows. Set Connection as Serial Port as well as Serial settings as regarded COM port where USB to RS-485 module is associated. At that point set the Baud rate as 115200 (As I utilized in Arduino Code), Data bits as 8, None Parity, 1 Stop Bits and Mode as RTU and afterward click OK.

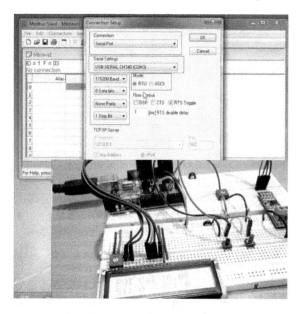

6. Note that No association vanishes and now open Setup->Slave Definition.

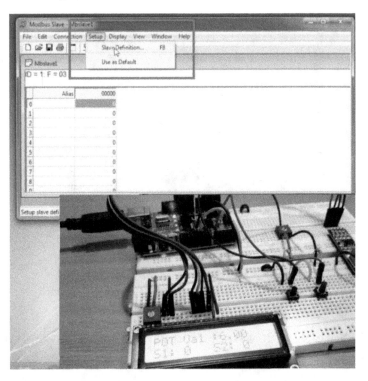

7. Presently enter the Slave ID as 1 and capacity as 03 Holding Register and address 0 and afterward click OK.

8. After that confirm the ID as 1 and F as 03. In this instructional exercise initial three registers are utilized (0-Potentiomter ADC value,1-Push catch value,2-Push catch esteem).

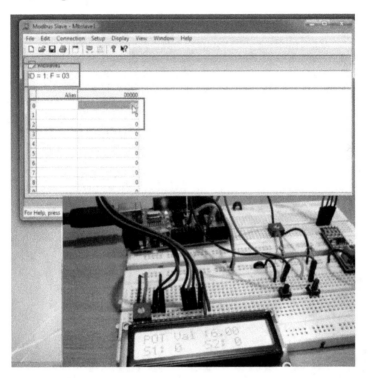

9. Presently when Push catch 2 is squeezed. Note the worth 1 in the third push. As push catch 1 isn't squeezed it stays 0 in second push and in first push some pot worth is shown.

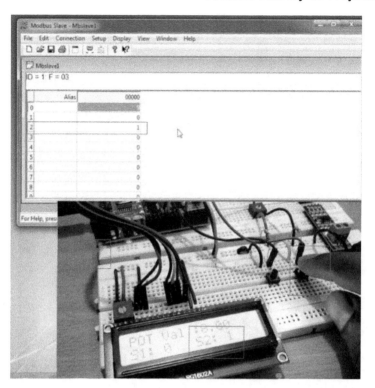

10. At the point when Push catch 1 is squeezed. Note the worth 1 in the subsequent column. What's more, as push catch 2 isn't squeezed so it stays 0 in third push and in first push some pot worth is shown.

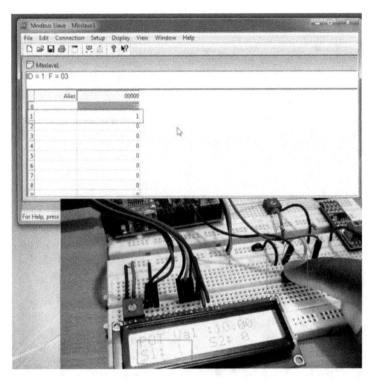

11. Presently when both the Push Buttons are Pressed, there are esteem 1 in the two columns second and third and furthermore note the potentiometer esteem.

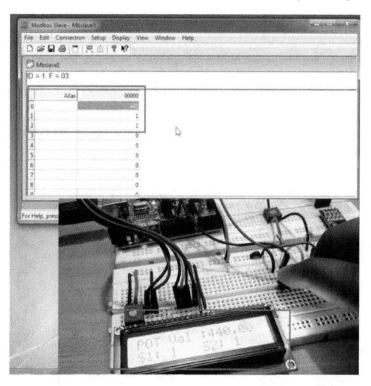

12. At the point when potentiometer is changed, the Row 1 likewise differs in the Modbus Slave programming.

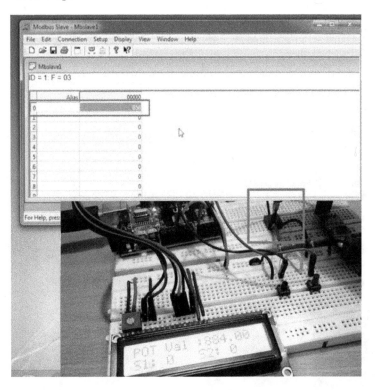

This is the means by which a RS-485 Modbus can be utilized in sequential correspondence with the Arduino UNO as Master. Check the past instructional exercise to see Arduino Uno as slave in MODBUS condemnation.

Locate the total code beneath

Code

```
#include <ModbusMaster.h>        //Library for using
```

```
ModbusMaster
#include <LiquidCrystal.h>        //Library for using
LCD display
#define MAX485_DE    3
#define MAX485_RE_NEG 2

ModbusMaster node;               //object node for class
ModbusMaster

LiquidCrystal lcd(8,9,10,11,12,13); //Object lcd for
class Liquidcrystal with LCD pins (RS, E, D4, D5, D6,
D7) that are connected with Arduino UNO.

void preTransmission()          //Function for setting
stste of Pins DE & RE of RS-485
{
 digitalWrite(MAX485_RE_NEG, 1);
 digitalWrite(MAX485_DE, 1);
}
void postTransmission()
{
 digitalWrite(MAX485_RE_NEG, 0);
 digitalWrite(MAX485_DE, 0);
}
void setup()
{
 lcd.begin(16,2);
 lcd.print("Hello_world");
 delay(3000);
 lcd.clear();
 lcd.print("Arduino");
 lcd.setCursor(0,1);
 lcd.print("Modbus Master");
```

```
delay(3000);
lcd.clear();


pinMode(MAX485_RE_NEG, OUTPUT);
pinMode(MAX485_DE, OUTPUT);


pinMode(4,INPUT);
pinMode(5,INPUT);


digitalWrite(MAX485_RE_NEG, 0);
digitalWrite(MAX485_DE, 0);
Serial.begin(115200);        //Baud Rate as 115200
node.begin(1, Serial);       //Slave ID as 1
node.preTransmission(preTransmission);    //Call-
back for configuring RS-485 Transreceiver correctly
node.postTransmission(postTransmission);
}
void loop()
{
float value = analogRead(A0);


node.writeSingleRegister(0x40000,value);          //
Writes value to 0x40000 holding register


lcd.setCursor(0,0);
lcd.print("POT Val :");
```

```
lcd.print(value);
int a= digitalRead(4);              //Reads state of push
button
int b= digitalRead(5);
if(a == 1)
{
node.writeSingleRegister(0x40001,1);        //Writes
1 to 0x40001 holding register
lcd.setCursor(0,1);
lcd.print("S1: 1");
}
else
{
node.writeSingleRegister(0x40001,0);        //Writes
0 to 0x40001 holding register
lcd.setCursor(0,1);
lcd.print("S1: 0");
}
if(b == 1)
{
node.writeSingleRegister(0x40002,1);        //Writes
1 to 0x40002 holding register
lcd.setCursor(8,1);
lcd.print("S2: 1");
}
else
{
  node.writeSingleRegister(0x40002,0);              //
Writes 0 to 0x40002 holding register
lcd.setCursor(8,1);
lcd.print("S2: 0");
```

Anbazhagan k

}

}

4.HOW TO USE HM-10 BLE MODULE WITH ARDUINO TO CONTROL AN LED USING ANDROID APP

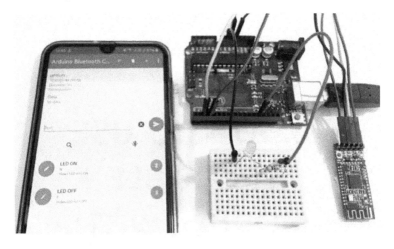

Bluetooth is the most prevalent and simple to utilize remote innovation. Over two years there are numerous updates of Bluetooth standard to keep pace with the current progressing innovation with future innovation and to fulfill needs of clients. Beginning from the Bluetooth rendition 1.0 to Bluetooth variant 5.0, there are numerous things changed including higher information rates, the capacity to be utilized for IoT with low current utilization, improved security, and so forth. To learn Bluetooth correspondence there are numerous modules accessible which can be interfaced with microcontrollers. Such a Bluetooth module is HM10 which depends on Bluetooth 4.0.

What is HM10 BLE 4.0 Module?

The HM10 is a sequential BLE module (Bluetooth-Low-Energy) which is proposed to use for the low control utilization applications and can keep going long even with a coin-sized battery. The HM10 is a Bluetooth 4.0 module dependent on the Texas Instruments CC2540 or CC2541 BLE System SoC. The firmware and plan of the module is made as well as overseen by Jinan Huamao Technology. The module accompanies sequential/UART layer which makes the gadget to have the option to interface with different microcontrollers. The HM10 is perfect for making straightforward associations and utilizing it with or as an iBeacon.

The HM10 has turned into a mainstream Bluetooth

4.0 BLE module. The HM10 is a Bluetooth 4.0 based module just, so it won't associate with Bluetooth 2/2.1 module, for example, HC-05, HC-06 and other Bluetooth modules. The HM10 is controlled by means of AT directions sent over the sequential UART association. HM-10 is a BLE module, to find out about BLE pursue the connection. Likewise figure out how a nRF24L01 module can be utilized as BLE module with Arduino.

Difference between HM10 and other Bluetooth Module

The significant contrast HM10 have is the Bluetooth Version. The HM10 is Bluetooth 4.0 module, so it accompanies all Bluetooth Edition 4.0 highlights, for example, speed, throughput and range. The HM10 offers an information pace of up to 24 Mbps with low-vitality/low-control utilization. Alongside this the HM10 offers a separation scope of 100 meters in open space. Contrast with other Bluetooth modules, for example, HC-05 which is a Bluetooth 2.0 based module, the HM10 surely performs superior to the HC-05. The HC-05 just offers 3 Mbps contrasted with HM10 which is very less.

Bluetooth module HC-05 and HC-06 are still exceptionally famous among producers and specialists as they are shoddy and simple to interface. We additionally made numerous activities utilizing HC-05/06 and interfaced them with numerous different microcontrollers:

1. Bluetooth Module Interfacing with ESP8266: Controlling a LED

2. Interfacing Bluetooth HC-05 with STM32F103C8 Blue Pill: Controlling LED

3. Interfacing HC-05 Bluetooth module with AVR Microcontroller

4. Interfacing Bluetooth Module HC-06 with PIC Microcontroller

5. Voice Controlled LEDs utilizing Arduino and Bluetooth

6. Voice Controlled Lights utilizing Raspberry Pi

All the Bluetooth related tasks can be found at this connection.

Today we will interface HM-10 BLE Module with Arduino Uno to manage a LED remotely utilizing Bluetooth convention. The On/Off directions will be sent by Smartphone.

Components Required

Hardware:

- Arduino UNO
- HM10 Bluetooth Module
- Resistors(1 kO, 470 O)
- Jumper Wires

Software:

- Arduino Bluetooth Controller(HM-10 Module) Android App
- Arduino IDE
- Android Smart phone

Circuit Diagram

Circuit outline for interfacing Arduino and HM-10 Bluetooth module is extremely straightforward as demonstrated as follows.

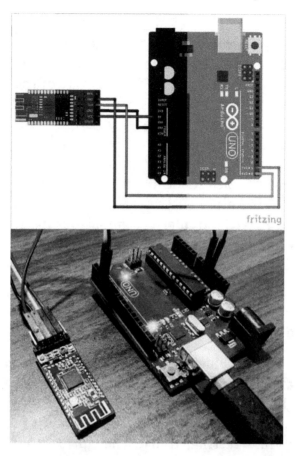

Before beginning with the undertaking ensure that your HM-10 module is a veritable HM-10 module. There are generally Chinese cloned HM-10 modules accessible. To distinguish the contrast among Genuine and Cloned HM-10 module, simply look the nearness of Crystal Oscillator of 32KHz on the HM-10 Board. In the event that the Crystal Oscillator is available, at that point it is a certifiable HM-10 Module and you don't have to change the Firmware. Be that as it may, in case you can't see the Crystal Oscillator instead of it, at that point it is a Cloned HM10 module and you have to change the Firmware of the Cloned HM-10 Module. Without changing the HM-10 firmware, you can neither access the HM-10 module with AT directions nor you can match it with cell phones. Here we are additionally utilizing the clone module so we flashed its firmware previously interfacing it with Ardruino. So as to change the Firmware of Cloned HM-10 module, just pursue our instructional exercise on How to change or blaze the Firmware of Clone HM-10 module.

Arduino Bluetooth Controller (HM-10 Module) Android Application

The Arduino Bluetooth Controller (HM-10 Module) is a android application which is accessible free on Google Play Store. This application is having simple and straightforward interface for HM-10 BLE Module. While testing, it had the option to discover HM-10 rapidly and it associated in a split second with HM-10. The application has some cool component like you can make a catch and tweak it with custom name and capacities. Here we will how to make two catches in this Bluetooth controller application to kill on and the LED associated with Arduino.

How to setup Arduino Bluetooth Controller (HM-10 Module) Android App:

Download the application from Google Play Store.

 Arduino Bluetooth
Controller (HM-10
Module)
Argon Dev

Tools

- The Home page of the application will look like underneath where you can discover highlights like, associate Device, Search Icon, Delete Icon, Device Status, Send Text, Add Template and so forth. Begin with looking through the Device either by tapping on Search Icon or by clicking to three dabs on the upright corner as well as pick associate Device.

Anbazhagan k

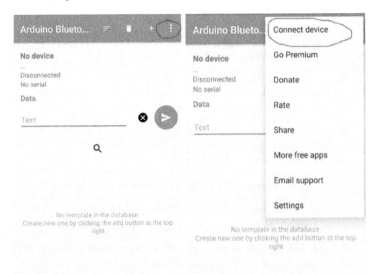

- Every single accessible gadget will be appeared in the screen. Pick the right HM-10 Module.

- Presently the HM-10 will be effectively associated and you will most likely observe the status of HM-10 in the Top of Screen.

Anbazhagan k

- Presently possibly you can straightforwardly send a content or String by composing on the content segment and hit bolt to send or you can make a custom format.

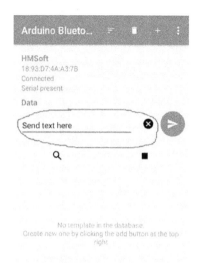

- To make a custom layout to spare time. Snap on the "+" symbol on upright corner and fill the subtleties. The "Name" is catch name, the "Content" field is for writings or string which will be sent to HM-10 and "Portrayal" is only the catch depiction that how the catch will work.

Anbazhagan k

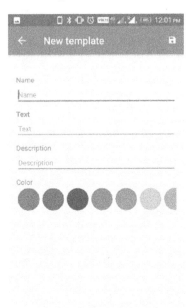

- Right off the bat, make a catch for turn LED ON and give it a Green Color. The Button will send "N" letter to HM-10 which will turn on the LED associated with Arduino. Also make a catch for LED OFF and give it a Red Color. . The Button will send "F" letter to HM-10 which will mood killer the LED associated with Arduino.

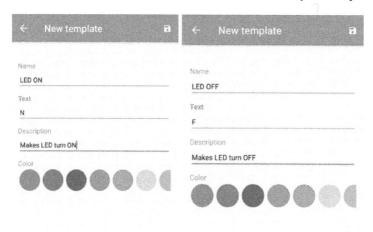

- Presently you can see the two catches made just beneath the Text Field. Presently on the off chance that you need to control LED, at that point simply click on the Buttons.

Anbazhagan k

This wraps the setting up android application to manage the HM-10 module. Presently we will begin with the programming Arduino Uno to get the characters from Android App.

Programming Arduino UNO to Control LED using HM-10 Bluetooth Module

Programming Arduino UNO for this venture neither requires much exertion nor any library. You can utilize equipment sequential and programming sequential library. In case that you are utilizing programming sequential, at that point simply incorporate programming sequential library else continue with equipment sequential. In this task we are utilizing SoftwareSerial. So begin with including Software Serial Library. The pins Rx and Tx are associated at 2 and 3 Pins of Arduino.

```
#include <SoftwareSerial.h>

SoftwareSerial HM10(2, 3); // RX = 2, TX = 3
```

The two factors are utilized to store the information got from HM10 and android application.

```
char appData;

String inData = "";
```

Simply begin the Hardware and Software Serial at 9600 baud rate and print some investigating explanations. The LED stick is set as yield and at first it is off.

```
Serial.begin(9600);

  Serial.println("HM10 serial started at 9600");

  HM10.begin(9600); // set HM10 serial at 9600
baud rate

  pinMode(13, OUTPUT); // onboard LED
```

```
digitalWrite(13, LOW); // switch OFF LED
```

Begin listening the HM10 port and read the string until the HM10 is accessible and sends the information. Spare the information in string.

```
HM10.listen(); // listen the HM10 port

  while (HM10.available() > 0) { // if HM10 sends
something then read

    appData = HM10.read();

    inData = String(appData);  // save the data in
string format

    Serial.write(appData);

  }
```

For troubleshooting the HM10 with AT directions simply compose the beneath code line which will send the string to HM10.

```
if (Serial.available()) {        // Read user input if
available.

  delay(10);
```

```
HM10.write(Serial.read());

}
```

On the off chance that the got string is "F" at that point print a message on sequential screen and mood killer the drove else on the off chance that the got string is "N" at that point print a message on sequential screen and Blink drove with a postponement of 500ms.

```
if ( inData == "F") {

    Serial.println("LED OFF");

    digitalWrite(13, LOW); // switch OFF LED

    delay(500);

}

if ( inData == "N") {

    Serial.println("LED ON");

    digitalWrite(13, HIGH); // switch OFF LED

    delay(500);
```

```
digitalWrite(13, LOW); // switch OFF LED

delay(500);

}
```

This completes the total instructional exercise on the most proficient method to control LED utilizing Arduino and BLE HM10 Blutooth 4.0 module. Again recollect that, in case you have a veritable HM10 module, at that point you did not need to streak its firmware, it very well may be utilized straight away. In any case, If you are utilizing a cloned HM-10 module at that point streak the firmware on clone HM10

BLE module.

Code

```
#include <SoftwareSerial.h>
SoftwareSerial HM10(2, 3); // RX = 2, TX = 3
char appData;
String inData = "";
void setup()
{
 Serial.begin(9600);
 Serial.println("HM10 serial started at 9600");
  HM10.begin(9600); // set HM10 serial at 9600 baud
rate
 pinMode(13, OUTPUT); // onboard LED
 digitalWrite(13, LOW); // switch OFF LED
}
void loop()
{
 HM10.listen(); // listen the HM10 port
  while (HM10.available() > 0) {   // if HM10 sends
something then read
  appData = HM10.read();
   inData = String(appData); // save the data in string
format
  Serial.write(appData);
 }


  if (Serial.available()) {      // Read user input if avail-
```

```
able.
 delay(10);
 HM10.write(Serial.read());
 }
 if( inData == "F") {
 Serial.println("LED OFF");
 digitalWrite(13, LOW); // switch OFF LED
 delay(500);
 }
 if( inData == "N") {
 Serial.println("LED ON");
 digitalWrite(13, HIGH); // switch OFF LED
 delay(500);
 digitalWrite(13, LOW); // switch OFF LED
 delay(500);
 }
}
```

5.JOYSTICK GAME CONTROLLER USING ARDUINO LEONARDO

We beforehand interfaced Joystick with Arduino UNO to see how it functions and controlled four LEDs to its left side, appropriate, all over development. In this venture we will utilize a similar Joystick as Gamepad or game controller to play any PC games which requires left, appropriate, all over developments. To mess around which requies more control choices, at least two joysticks can be utilized. Here we will utilize Arduino Leonardo to interface Joystick as Game controller. Arduino Leonardo has advantage over Uno that we can introduce USB drivers on it and it tends to be distinguished as mouse, console or joystick by PC when associated.

Components Required

1. Dual Axis XY Joystick Module
2. Arduino Leonardo
3. Connecting wires
4. Arduino IDE

Arduino Leonardo

For this task we are utilizing the Arduino Leonardo, it is a microcontroller board dependent on the AT-mega32u4. It has 20 computerized input/yield pins (out of which 7 can be used as PWM yields and 12 as Analog information sources), a 16 MHz precious stone oscillator, a small scale USB association, a power jack, an ICSP header as well as a reset catch. It contains everything to help the microcontroller just interface it to a pc with a usb connection or power it with an air conditioner to dc connector or battery to start.

The Leonardo is not quite the same as every first board in that the ATmega32u4 has worked in USB correspondence, taking out the requirement for an auxiliary processor. This enables the Leonardo to appear to an associated PC as a mouse as well as console, notwithstanding a virtual (CDC) sequential/COM port.

Technical Specifications

Microcontroller	ATmega32u4
Operating Voltage	5V
Input Voltage (Recommended)	7-12V
Input Voltage (limits)	6-20V
Digital I/O Pins	20

PWM Channels	7
Analog Input Channels	12
DC Current per I/O Pin	40 mA
DC Current for 3.3V Pin	50 mA
Flash Memory	32 KB (ATmega32u4) of which 4 KB used by bootloader
SRAM	2.5 KB (ATmega32u4)
EEPROM	1 KB (ATmega32u4)
Clock Speed	16 MHz
Length	68.6 mm
Width	53.3 mm
Weight	20 g

PIN Out Reference

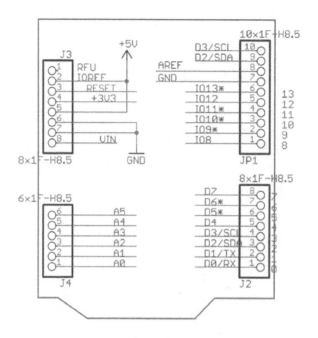

Dual Axis XY Joystick Module

Joysticks are accessible in various shapes as well as sizes. A regular Joystick module is appeared in the figure beneath. This Joystick module normally gives Analog Outputs and the yield voltages given by this module continue altering as indicated by the course in which we move it. What's more, we get the heading of development by deciphering these voltage changes utilizing some microcontroller. Beforehand we interfaced euphoria stick with various microcontrollers:

1. Interfacing Joystick with Arduino

2. Interfacing Joystick with Raspberry Pi

3. Interfacing Joystick with PIC Microcontroller

4. Joystick Interfacing with AVR Microcontroller

This joystick module has two tomahawks as should be obvious. They are X-pivot and Y-hub. Every hub of JOY STICK is mounted to a potentiometer or pot. The mid purposes of these pots are driven out as Rx and Ry. So Rx and Ry are variable focuses to these pots. At the point when the Joystick is in backup, Rx and Ry go about as voltage divider.

At the point when joystick is moved along the level hub, the voltage at Rx stick changes. So also, when it is moved along the vertical pivot, the voltage at Ry stick changes. So we have four headings of Joystick on two ADC yields. At the point when the stick is moved, the voltage on each stick goes high or low contingent upon course.

Circuit Diagram

This Arduino Joystick Game Controller requires associations between the Arduino and the Joystick as pursues:

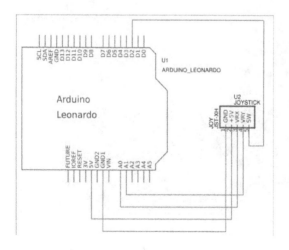

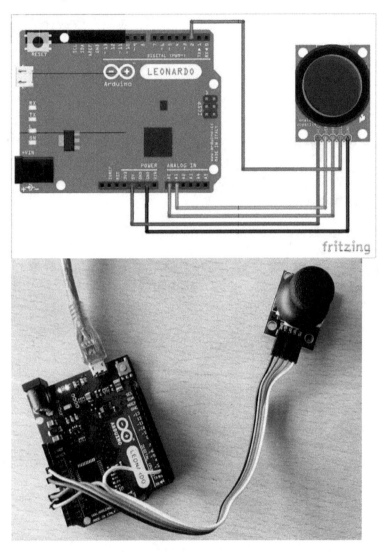

Code and Working Explanation

Right off the bat, we have to instate the console

library

> **#include<Keyboard.h>**

Next in beneath code, we have initialised X and Y pivot of the Joystick module for Analog stick A0 and A1 separately.

> **const int X_pin and const int Y_pin respectively**

The simple estimation of the VRX stick is perused and on the off chance that the worth is 1023, at that point the direction for "up" is given and on the off chance that the worth is 0, at that point the order for "down" is given.

Thus, the simple estimation of the VRY stick is perused and in the event that the worth is 1023, at that point the order for "right" is given and on the off chance that the worth is 0, at that point the direction for "left" is given.

Joystick additionally has a push catch on top so this catch (SW) is likewise perused and in the event that the catch is squeezed the worth will be 0, at that point the direction for "enter" is given.

At long last consume the code into Arduino and interface the Arduino with PC.

Next check the 'Gadgets and Printers' in your control board, you will probably observe "Arduino Leonardo" under gadgets segment as appeared in beneath picture. Presently you are prepared to play with the joystick.

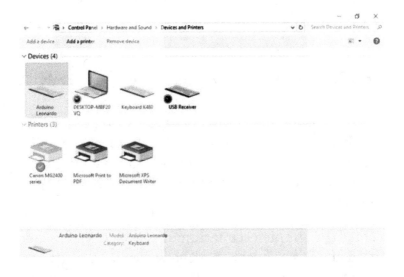

We can control any game controls utilizing this Joystick. The Joystick has two potentiometers inside it, one is for X-pivot development and another is for Y-hub development. Every potentiometer gets 5v from the Arduino. So as we move the joystick, the voltage worth will change and the simple incentive at Analog pins A0 as well as A1 will likewise change. So the joystick will go about as a gamepad.

So this is the manner by which a typical Joystick can be changed over into a Game Controller utilizing Arduino Leonardo and can be utilized to mess around having every one of the controls to move left, ideal, here and there. As told earliar beyond what one Joystick can be interfaced to get a greater number of controls other than these fundamental four capacities.

Code

```
#include<Keyboard.h>
const int SW_pin = 2; // digital pin connected to switch output
const int X_pin = A0; // analog pin connected to X
```

```
output
const int Y_pin = A1; // analog pin connected to Y
output
int x, y;
void setup()
{
 pinMode(SW_pin, INPUT); // SW pin set as input
 digitalWrite(SW_pin, HIGH); // A high value is writ-
ten to SW pin
 Serial.begin(115200);
 Keyboard.begin();
}
void loop()
{
 x = analogRead(X_pin); // output of X_pin is read
 if(x == 1023) // check whether the value of x = 1023
 {
  Serial.println("Up:");
  Keyboard.press(218); // key moves up
 }
 else
 {
  Keyboard.release(218); // release the key
 }
 x = analogRead(X_pin); // output of X_pin is read
 if(x == 0) // check whether the value of x = 0
 {
  Serial.println("Down:");
  Keyboard.press(217); // key moves down
 }
 else
```

```
{
 Keyboard.release(217); // release the key
}
y = analogRead(Y_pin); // output of Y_pin is read
  if (y == 1023) // check whether the value of y =
1023
 {
  Serial.println("Right:");
  Keyboard.press(216); // key moves right
 }
 else
 {
 Keyboard.release(216); // release the key
 }
y = analogRead(Y_pin); // output of Y_pin is read
  if (y == 0) // check whether the value of y = 0
 {
  Serial.println("Left:");
  Keyboard.press(215); // key moves left
 }
else
{
 Keyboard.release(215); // release the key
}
 int z = digitalRead(SW_pin); // read the value of SW
pin
  if (z == 0) //check whether the value of z = 0
 {
  Serial.println("Enter:");
  Keyboard.println(); //enter key is pressed
```

Anbazhagan k

```
 }
 delay(500);
}
```

◆ ◆ ◆

6.DIY ARDUINO BASED COLOR SORTER MACHINE USING TCS3200 COLOR SENSOR

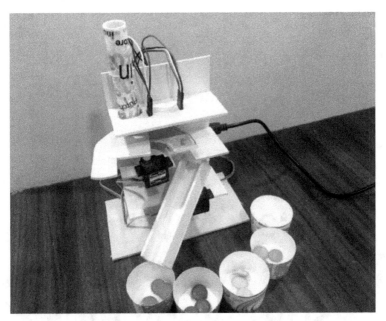

As the name proposes, shading arranging is essentially to sort the things as indicated by their shading. It tends to be effectively done by observing it yet when there are an excessive number of things to be arranged and it is a tedious errand then programmed shading arranging machines are helpful. These machines have shading sensor to detect the shade of any items and subsequent to recognizing the shading servo engine snatch the thing and put it into separate box. They can be utilized in various application regions where shading recognizable proof, shading qualification and shading arranging is significant. A portion of the application zones incorporate Agriculture Industry (Grain Sorting based on shading), Food Industry, Diamond and Mining Industry, Recycling and so on. The applications are not restricted to this and can be additionally connected to various businesses.

Most well known sensor for identifying the hues is TCS3200 shading sensor. We recently utilized TCS3200 sensor with Arduino to get the RGB part of any shading and furthermore interfaced it with Raspberry Pi for recognizing the shade of any item.

Here in this instructional exercise we will make a shading arranging machine utilizing a shading sensor TCS3200, some servo engines and Arduino board. This instructional exercise will incorporate the arranging of hued balls and keeping them in the applicable shading box. The container will be in the fixed position and the servo engine will be utilized to move the sorter hand to keep the ball in the pertinent box.

Components Required

     1. Arduino UNO
     2. TCS3200 Color Sensor
     3. Servo Motors
     4. Jumpers
     5. Breadboard

How to make the chassis for Color Sorting Robotic Arm

For making the total arrangement including body, arm, roller, cushion, we have utilized the white Sunboard of 2mm thickness. It is effectively accessible in the stationary stores. We have utilized paper shaper to cut the Sunboard Sheet and FlexKwik or FeviKwik for joining the various parts.

The following are a few stages fabricate the Color arranging Arm:

1) Take the Sunboard Sheet.

2) Cut the sunboard sheet into pieces subsequent to estimating all sides with scale and marker as ap-

peared in the figure.

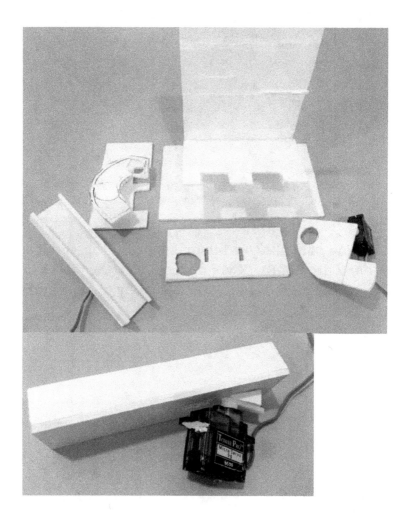

3) Now hold the two bits of sunboard together and pour a drop of FeviKwik on it to stick the pieces together. Continue joining the pieces by following the figure.

4) After combining every one of the pieces, this shading arranging machine will look something like this:

Anbazhagan k

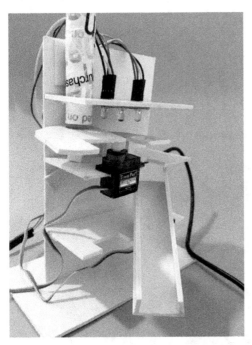

TCS3200 Color Sensor

TCS3200 is a shading sensor which can recognize any number of hues with right programming. TCS3200 contains RGB exhibits. As appeared in figure on minuscule level one can see the square boxes inside the eye on sensor. These square boxes are varieties of RGB framework. Each of these crates contain three sensors, One is for detecting RED light power, One is for detecting GREEN light force and the toward the end in for detecting BLUE light power.

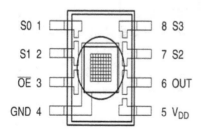

Every one of sensor exhibits in these three clusters are chosen independently relying upon the prerequisite. Thus it is known as programmable sensor. The module can be included to detect the specific shading and to leave the others. It contains channels for that determination reason. There is a forward mode called 'no channel mode' where the sensor recognizes white light.

Circuit Diagram

The circuit graph for this Arduino Color Sorter is truly simple to make and doesn't require much associations. The schematic is given underneath.

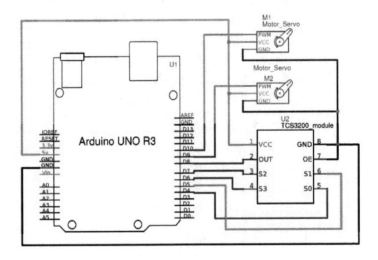

This is the hardware behind the arrangement of shading arranging machine:

Programming Arduino Uno for sorting colourful balls

Programing Arduino UNO is a really straightforward and requires a basic rationale to improve the means associated with shading arranging.

Since the servo engine is utilized, so the servo library is fundamental piece of the program. Here we are utilizing two servo engines. The primary servo will move the hued balls from introductory position to TCS3200 finder position and afterward move to the arranging position where the ball will be dropped. Subsequent to moving to arranging position, the subsequent servo will fail utilizing its arm to the ideal shading basin.

The initial step will be all library incorporation and characterize the servo factors.

```
#include <Servo.h>

Servo pickServo;

Servo dropServo;
```

The TCS3200 shading sensor can work without library as there is just need of perusing recurrence from sensor stick to choose the shading. So simply characterize the stick quantities of TCS3200.

```
#define S0 4

#define S1 5

#define S2 7

#define S3 6
```

```
#define sensorOut 8

int frequency = 0;

int color=0;
```

Make the select sticks as yield as this will make the shading photodiode high or low and take the Out stick of TCS3200 as info. The OUT stick will give recurrence. Select the scaling of recurrence as 20% at first.

```
pinMode(S0, OUTPUT);

  pinMode(S1, OUTPUT);

  pinMode(S2, OUTPUT);

  pinMode(S3, OUTPUT);

  pinMode(sensorOut, INPUT);

  digitalWrite(S0, LOW);

  digitalWrite(S1, HIGH);
```

The servo engines are associated at Pin 9 and 10 of Arduino. The pickup servo which will pickup the shading balls is associated at Pin 9 and the drop servo which will drop the shading balls as indicated by the shading is associated at Pin10.

```
pickServo.attach(9);

dropServo.attach(10);
```

At first the pick servo engine is set in the at first position which for this situation is 115 degrees. It might vary and can be modified as needs be. The engine moves after some deferral to the identifier area and sits tight for the recognition.

```
pickServo.write(115);

delay(600);

for(int i = 115; i > 65; i--){

  pickServo.write(i);

  delay(2);

}

delay(500);
```

The TCS 3200 peruses the shading and gives the recurrence from the Out Pin.

```
color = detectColor();

delay(1000);
```

Contingent On the shading identified, the drop servo engine moves with specific point and drops the shading ball to its particular box.

```
switch (color) {

    case 1:

    dropServo.write(50);

    break;

    case 2:

    dropServo.write(80);

    break;

    case 3:

    dropServo.write(110);
```

```
    break;

    case 4:

    dropServo.write(140);

    break;

    case 5:

    dropServo.write(170);

    break;

    case 0:

    break;

}

delay(500);
```

The servo engine comes back to the underlying position for the following ball to pick.

```
for(int i = 65; i > 29; i--){

    pickServo.write(i);
```

```
  delay(2);

}

delay(300);

for(int i = 29; i < 115; i++){

  pickServo.write(i);

  delay(2);

}
```

The capacity detectColor() is utilized to quantify recurrence and looks at the shading recurrence to make the finish of shading. The outcome is imprinted on the sequential screen. At that point it restores the shading an incentive for cases to move the drop servo engine edge.

```
int detectColor() {
```

Writing to S2 and S3 (LOW,LOW) actuates the red photodiodes to take the readings for red shading thickness.

```
digitalWrite(S2, LOW);
```

```
digitalWrite(S3, LOW);

frequency = pulseIn(sensorOut, LOW);

int R = frequency;

Serial.print("Red = ");

Serial.print(frequency);//printing RED color fre-
quency

Serial.print(" ");

delay(50);
```

Writing to S2 and S3 (LOW,HIGH) initiates the blue photodiodes to take the readings for blue shading thickness.

```
digitalWrite(S2, LOW);

digitalWrite(S3, HIGH);

frequency = pulseIn(sensorOut, LOW);

int B = frequency;

Serial.print("Blue = ");
```

```
Serial.print(frequency);

Serial.println(" ");
```

Writing to S2 and S3 (HIGH,HIGH) enacts the green photodiodes to take the readings for green shading thickness.

```
digitalWrite(S2, HIGH);

digitalWrite(S3, HIGH);

// Reading the output frequency

frequency = pulseIn(sensorOut, LOW);

int G = frequency;

Serial.print("Green = ");

Serial.print(frequency);

Serial.print("  ");

delay(50);
```

At this point the qualities are contrasted with settle on the shading choice. The readings are distinctive for various trial arrangement as the location separation changes for everybody when making the arrangement.

```
if(R<22 & R>20 & G<29 & G>27){

  color = 1; // Red

  Serial.print("Detected Color is = ");

  Serial.println("RED");

}

if(G<25 & G>22 & B<22 &B>19){

  color = 2; // Orange

    Serial.println("Orange ");

}

if(R<21 & R>20 & G<28 & G>25){

  color = 3; // Green

    Serial.print("Detected Color is = ");

  Serial.println("GREEN");
```

```
}

if(R<38 & R>24 & G<44 & G>30){

  color = 4; // Yellow

    Serial.print("Detected Color is = ");

  Serial.println("YELLOW");

}

if (G<29 & G>27 & B<22 &B>19){

  color = 5; // Blue

    Serial.print("Detected Color is = ");

  Serial.println("BLUE");

}

  return color;

}
```

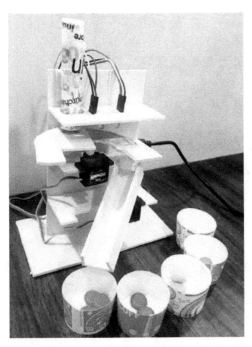

This completes the shading arranging machine utilizing TCS3200 and Arduino UNO. You can likewise program it to distinguish more hues if necessary.

Code

```
#include <Servo.h>
Servo pickServo;
Servo dropServo;
#define S0 4
#define S1 5
#define S2 7
```

```
#define S3 6
#define sensorOut 8
int frequency = 0;
int color=0;
int detectColor() {
 // activating red photodiodes to read
 digitalWrite(S2, LOW);
 digitalWrite(S3, LOW);
 frequency = pulseIn(sensorOut, LOW);
 int R = frequency;
 Serial.print("Red = ");
   Serial.print(frequency);//printing RED color fre-
quency
 Serial.print(" ");
 delay(50);
   // activating blue photodiodes to read
 digitalWrite(S2, LOW);
 digitalWrite(S3, HIGH);
 frequency = pulseIn(sensorOut, LOW);
 int B = frequency;
 Serial.print("Blue = ");
 Serial.print(frequency);
 Serial.println(" ");


  // activating green photodiodes to read
 digitalWrite(S2, HIGH);
 digitalWrite(S3, HIGH);
 // Reading the output frequency
 frequency = pulseIn(sensorOut, LOW);
 int G = frequency;
```

```
Serial.print("Green = ");
Serial.print(frequency);
Serial.print(" ");
delay(50);
 delay(50);
//Readings are different for different setup
//change the readings according your project and
readings detected
if(R<22 & R>20 & G<29 & G>27){
 color = 1; // Red
 Serial.print("Detected Color is = ");
 Serial.println("RED");
}
if(G<25 & G>22 & B<22 &B>19){
 color = 2; // Orange
  Serial.println("Orange ");
}
if(R<21 & R>20 & G<28 & G>25){
 color = 3; // Green
  Serial.print("Detected Color is = ");
 Serial.println("GREEN");
}
if(R<38 & R>24 & G<44 & G>30){
 color = 4; // Yellow
  Serial.print("Detected Color is = ");
 Serial.println("YELLOW");
}
if(G<29 & G>27 & B<22 &B>19){
 color = 5; // Blue
  Serial.print("Detected Color is = ");
```

```
  Serial.println("BLUE");
 }
 return color;
}
void setup() {
 pinMode(S0, OUTPUT);
 pinMode(S1, OUTPUT);
 pinMode(S2, OUTPUT);
 pinMode(S3, OUTPUT);
 pinMode(sensorOut, INPUT);
  //frequency-scaling to 20% selected
 digitalWrite(S0, LOW);
 digitalWrite(S1, HIGH);
  pickServo.attach(9);
 dropServo.attach(10);
  Serial.begin(9600);
}
void loop() {
 //initial position of servo motor
 pickServo.write(115);
 delay(600);


  for(int i = 115; i > 65; i--) {
  pickServo.write(i);
  delay(2);
 }
 delay(500);
  //read color values by calling function. save the
values for conclusion in variable
```

```
color = detectColor();
delay(1000);
 switch(color){
 case 1:
 dropServo.write(50);


   break;
   case 2:
 dropServo.write(80);
 break;
   case 3:
 dropServo.write(110);
 break;
   case 4:
 dropServo.write(140);
 break;
   case 5:
 dropServo.write(170);
 break;


   case 0:
 break;
 }
 delay(500);


 for(int i = 65; i > 29; i--){
 pickServo.write(i);
 delay(2);
```

```
}
delay(300);


for(int i = 29; i < 115; i++){
pickServo.write(i);
delay(2);
}
color=0;
}
```

Anbazhagan k

7.SENDING SENSOR DATA TO ANDROID PHONE USING ARDUINO AND NRF24L01 OVER BLUETOOTH (BLE)

B LE is an adaptation of Bluetooth and it is available as a littler, exceptionally advanced variant of the exemplary Bluetooth. It is otherwise called Smart Bluetooth. The BLE was structured remembering the most minimal conceivable power utilization explicitly for ease, low data transfer capacity, low power and low intricacy. ESP32 has inbuilt BLE abilities yet for different microcontrollers like Arduino, nRF24L01 can be utilized. This RF module can be additionally utilized as BLE module to send the information to other Bluetooth gadget like cell phones, PC and so forth.

Here in this instructional exercise we will show how to send any information over BLE utilizing nRF24L01. We will send temperature readings from DHT11 to cell phone utilizing Arduino as well as nRF module over BLE.

How Bluetooth Low Energy (BLE) is different?

The BLE was received because of its capacity utilization includes as it had the option to keep running for an all-inclusive timeframe utilizing only a coin cell. Contrasted with different remote principles, the quick development of BLE has gone further quicker in light of its remarkable applications in cell phones, tablets, and versatile registering.

BLE Capability of NRF24L01 Module

BLE utilizes the equivalent 2.4 GHz ISM band with baud rate from 250Kbps to 2Mbps which is permitted in numerous nations and connected to mechanical and restorative applications. The Band begins at 2400 MHz to 2483.5 MHz as well as it is the isolated into 40 channels. Three of these channels are known as 'Publicizing' and are utilized by gadgets to send promoting bundles with data about them so other BLE gadgets can associate. These channels were at first chosen at the lower upper of the band and center of the band to keep away from obstruction which can meddle with various channels. To study BLE, pursue this instructional exercise.

This instructional exercise will disclose how to utilize NRF24L01 module as BLE handset. The instructional exercise on NRF24L01 as RF module has just been clarified in interfacing nRF24L01 with Arduino instructional exercise. Today the BLE usefulness of this module will be clarified by sending sensor information to an advanced mobile phone.This nRF24L01 module is interfaced with Arduino Microcontroller as well as the DHT11 sensor temperature information will be sent to official Nordic BLE android application.

Components Required

Hardware:

1. Arduino UNO
2. nRF24L01 BLE Module
3. DHT11 Temperature and Humidity Sensor
4. Jumpers

Software:

1. Arduino IDE
2. Nordic BLE Android Application (nRF Temp 2.0 for BLE or nRF Connect for Mobile)

Starting with nRF24L01 Module

The nRF24L01 modules are handset modules, which means every module can send as well as get information however they are half-duplex they can either send or get information at once. The module has the conventional nRF24L01 IC from Nordic semi-conductors which is in charge of transmission and gathering of information. The IC imparts utilizing the SPI convention and consequently can be effectively interfaced with any microcontrollers. It gets much simpler with Arduino since the libraries are promptly accessible. We officially utilized nRF24L01 module with Arduino to make a visit room and to control servo engines remotely.

The pinouts of a standard nRF24L01 module is demonstrated as follows:

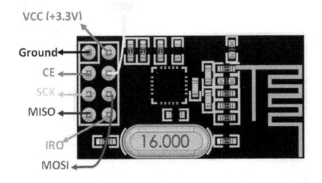

The module has on working voltage from 1.9V to 3.6V (ordinarily 3.3V) and devours less present of just 12mA during ordinary activity which makes it battery productive and consequently can even keep running on coin cells. Inspite the working voltage is 3.3V the greater part of the pins are 5V tolerant and henceforth can be straightforwardly interfaced with 5V microcontrollers like Arduino. Another favorable position of utilizing these modules is that, every module has 6 Pipelines. Which means, every module can speak with 6 different modules to transmit or get information. This makes the module appropriate for making star or work organizes in IoT applications. Likewise they have a wide address scope of 125 remarkable ID's, consequently in a shut territory we can utilize 125 of these modules without meddling with one another.

Arduino NRF24L01 Module **Circuit Diagram**

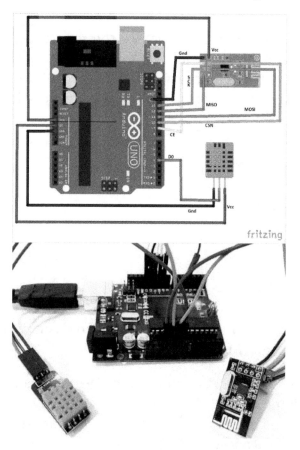

Interfacing nRF24L01 with Arduino for BLE communication

The nRF24L01 takes a shot at SPI, so the interfacing will utilize SPI Protocol. Here the nRF24L01 module is utilized to speak with Smartphone App of Nordic.

Right off the bat incorporate the required libraries. The library incorporates RF24 to get to nRF24L01 directions, DHT11 library for getting to DHT11 directions and BTLE library to utilize BLE capacities.

```
#include <SPI.h>

#include <RF24.h>

#include <BTLE.h>

#include <DHT.h>
```

Define and initialize the pins and functions for DHT11 and BLE module.

The DHT type is introduced as DHT11 since we are utilizing DHT11. The DHT is associated with GPIO Pin 4 and nRF module's CE and CSN pins are associated with Pin 9 and 10 individually.

```
#define DHTPIN

#define DHTTYPE DHT11

DHT22

DHT dht(DHTPIN, DHTTYPE);
```

```
RF24 radio(9, 10);

BTLE btle(&radio);
```

Begin the sequential port at 9600, you can pick any port. At that point start the DHT sensor and furthermore start BTLE with the Bluetooth Local Name with max 8 characters in length.

```
Serial.begin(9600);

dht.begin();

btle.begin("CD Temp");
```

Read the temperature over the loop and save it to a float variable *temp*. Include an investigate line for demonstrating a blunder message if DHT loses its capacity or anything startling occurs.

```
float temp = dht.readTemperature();  //read temperature data

 if (isnan(h) || isnan(t)) {

   Serial.println(F("Failed to read from DHT sensor!"));
```

```
  return;

}
```

Save the value to Buffer and parse it to the BLE module. Likewise send the Temperature incentive to BLE Module. The BLE module will promote the Temperature information. The android application can look through the BLE module and get the sensor information.

```
nrf_service_data buf;

 buf.service_uuid = NRF_TEMPERATURE_SER-
VICE_UUID;

 buf.value = BTLE::to_nRF_Float(temp);

 if (!btle.advertise(0x16, &buf, sizeof(buf))) {

  Serial.println("BTLE advertisement failed..!");

 }
```

Whenever done, simply bounce to the following channel.

```
 btle.hopChannel();
```

Since the DHT sensor documentation prescribes to keep a postponement of a base 2 seconds after one perusing, so include a deferral of 2 seconds.

```
delay(2000);
```

Subsequent to transferring the and matching the cell phone with nRF module, you will begin getting the qualities on nRF Temp 2.0 for BLE android application like demonstrated as follows.

This completes the total instructional exercise on promoting the sensor information to Nordic Android

Anbazhagan k

App utilizing BLE nRF24L01. To investigate increasingly about nRF24L02 , you can likewise attempt to make a Private Chat Room utilizing Arduino, nRF24L01 as well as Processing.

Code

```
/* Sending Sensor Data to Nordic BLE android app  by
works with nRF24L01. and the works for Nordic's
  It reads temperature from a DHT11 and sends it via
BTLE.
  Works with Nordic Semiconductor apps such as
  "nRF Connect for Mobile" and "nRF Temp 2.0 for BLE"
  Pin Mapping:
GND -> GND on the Arduino
VCC -> 3.3v on the Arduino
CE -> PIN 9 on the Arduino
CSN -> PIN 10 on the Arduino
SCK -> PIN 13 on the Arduino Uno
MOSI -> PIN 11 on the Arduino Uno
MISO -> PIN 12 on the Arduino Uno
IRQ -> not used
*/
#include <SPI.h>
#include <RF24.h>
#include <BTLE.h>
#include <DHT.h>                        // dht11 temperature and humidity sensor library
#define DHTPIN 4                        // what digital pin we're connected to
#define DHTTYPE DHT11                   // select
```

dht type as DHT 11 or DHT 22

```
DHT dht(DHTPIN, DHTTYPE);

RF24 radio(9, 10); // CE, CSN
BTLE btle(&radio);
void setup() {
 Serial.begin(9600);
 delay(1000);
 Serial.print("BLE and DHT Starting... ");
 Serial.println("Send Temperature Data over BTLE");
 dht.begin();  // initialise DHT 11 sensor
 btle.begin("CD Temp");  // 8 chars max
 Serial.println("Successfully Started");
}
void loop() {
  float temp = dht.readTemperature();   //read tem-
perature data
  if (isnan(h) || isnan(t)) {                      // Check if
any reads failed and exit early (to try again).
   Serial.println(F("Failed to read from DHT sensor!"));
   return;
}
  Serial.print(" Temperature: "); Serial.print(t); Ser-
ial.println("Â°C ");
 nrf_service_data buf;
    buf.service_uuid  =  NRF_TEMPERATURE_SER-
VICE_UUID;
 buf.value = BTLE::to_nRF_Float(temp);
  if (!btle.advertise(0x16, &buf, sizeof(buf))) {
  Serial.println("BTLE advertisement failed..!");
}
```

```
btle.hopChannel();
delay(2000);
}
```

8.PROGRAMMING ARDUINO USING PLATFORM IO

Platform IO

Advancement in Arduino and Arduino IDE has consistently been simple and fun with their straightforward UI. The Arduino IDE is open-source and allowed to utilize Development Environment with all highlights like compose, arrange and transfer the code to Arduino Boards. It depends on Java and keeps running on significant OS like Windows, OS X and Linux. Be that as it may, with all its effortlessness and enormous network, it doesn't have a few highlights which an accomplished designer will require for quick advancement that can lessen the improvement time frame. There are numerous advancement situations accessible for Arduino, yet all have a few focal points and hindrances. Today, we will begin with PlatformIO improvement condition which is anything but difficult to utilize and has added highlights contrast with Arduino condition.

What is PlatformIO?

The PlatformIO is a Python based open source biological system for IoT advancement and a cross stage IDE with a bound together debugger keeps running on Windows, Mac and Linux. PlatformIO accompanies library director for stages like Arduino or MBED support alongside unit testing and firmware refreshes. The PlatformIO underpins various Platforms, Frameworks, Boards like Arduino, ESP32, ESP8266 and accompanies number of models and libraries. It is free of the stage in which it is running and it requires just Python Installed on the PC.

Advantages of PlatformIO

The PlatformIO highlights quick advancement with its highlights like C/C++ Code Completion and Smart Code Linter for fast proficient improvement which isn't there in the Arduino IDE. Likewise, the PlatformIO offers the topic support with dull as well as light hues for advancement on whenever. It additionally accompanies Smart Code Navigations and Code Formatting. The center highlights incorporate the Multi-stage Build System, Library Manager, Serial Port Monitor and so forth.

The Unified Debugger with a help for the numerous structures and advancement stages permits to troubleshoot various implanted sheets with Zero-Configuration. The PlatformIO Unified Debugger has highlights like Conditional Breakpoints, Expressions and Watchpoints, Memory Viewer, A hot restart of a functioning troubleshooting session. The PlatformIO Core is wrote in Python 2.7 and takes a shot at Windows, macOS, Linux, FreeBSD and even ARM-based Visa measured PCs like Raspberry Pi, BeagleBone, CubieBoard, Samsung ARTIK, and so forth. Aside from this the PlatformIO has File Explorer which aides sorting out the records when the task develops to a specific level and arranging winds up essential.

Setting up PlatformIO for Arduino Uno

Utilizing PlatformIO is straightforward and requires few stages to begin. The PlatformIO requires Python introduced on the PC since as clarified over that the PlatformIO center was wrote in Python 2.7. Note that the PlatformIO does not bolster Python 3 so it is suggested that introduce Python 2 form and after that continue for setting up PlatformIO IDE. The PlatformIO is an IDE in addition to it gives authority bundles (modules, expansions) for the most prevalent IDEs and content managers.

Today we will introduce PlatformIO to such word processor like Atom and Visual Studio Code. In authority documentation of Platform IDE it expresses that the PlatformIO IDE for VS Code (Visual Studio Code) offers better framework execution, and clients have thought that it was simpler to begin. We want to set-up PlatformIO in Visual Studio Code. The VS Code is an outstanding content tool with number of expansions enabling us to create in various programming dialects.

How about we begin setting up the PlatformIO to begin creating code in Arduino UNO. There are steps included which are clarified underneath:

- Right off the bat introduce the Visual Studio Code from its official site. The establishment ventures of Visual Studio Code won't be clarified here yet you can discover it on VS Code site. There are general advances included simply like introducing some other programming on Windows OS.

- The Visual Studio Code will look like after when it is effectively introduced.

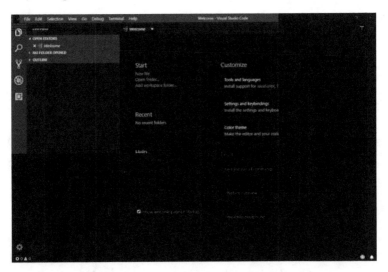

- Following stage incorporates introducing the PlatformIO utilizing VS Code Extensions. For this you need go to Extensions Icon on the upper left corner of the VS Code. There is square Box Icon which is the fifth symbol on the upper left corner. Simply click on that and one inquiry box will show up just next to that where you can discover numerous expansion for various programming dialects like C/C++, C#, Python, PHP, Go, JavaScript, TypeScript as well as Node.js and so on.

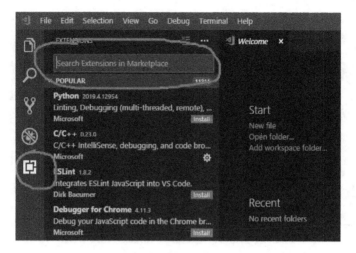

- Quest For "PlatformIO" in the expansion search box as well as you will notice PlatformIO Icon with Name as well as Description. Click it as well as Install it. It might require some investment introducing toolchains and different conditions. Conditions incorporate C/C++ condition as Arduino advancement is for most of the part done on C/C++.

- At the point when the establishment is finished, you will notice the accompanying interface. The Interface incorporates all the vital route, for example, making New Project, Import Arduino Project, Open Project, Project Examples and so on. It is prescribed to restart the VS Code Editor after the establishment of PlatformIO.

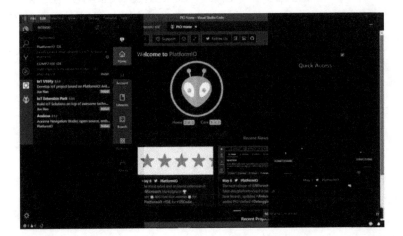

This completes the establishment ventures of PlatformIO. Presently the PlatformIO is introduced and prepared to utilize. Much the same as Arduino IDE, we will begin with the Blink Program and attempt to transfer the Blink Program in the Arduino UNO.

Programming Arduino UNO using the PlatformIO IDE

The PlatformIO interface will be clarified simultaneously while programming Arduino UNO. Here we are modifying Arduino for flickering LED utilizing the PlatformIO. The equivalent should be possible utilizing Arduino IDE. Pursue the beneath ventures underneath to make another undertaking for flickering LED.

- Select "New Project" tab from the speedy access menu.

- Name the undertaking (Here it is 'Squint'). Search as well as Select the board which is Arduino UNO. Since we are working in Arduino system, so the structure chosen will be Arduino. In the wake of filling all subtleties simply click on Finish.

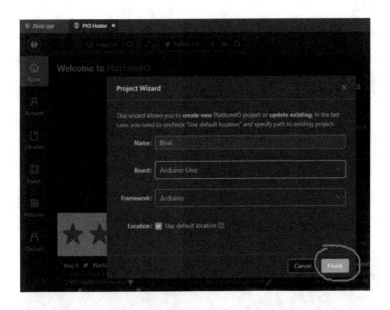

The Project will begin getting made by gathering assets and different conditions.

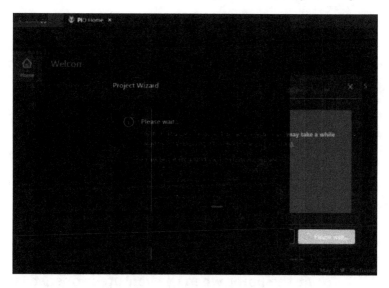

At the point when venture is effectively made, you will get the brief message as "Task has been effectively introduced" with every single filled detail.

- To open the made task, simply look down the Home Menu of PlatformIO and you will see all rundown of the ventures made from starting. At the correct corner of made task click on 'Open' to open the venture and begin altering.

- At the point when the venture is opened, at first it will resemble its covered up, yet don't stress, the PlatformIO has document traveler highlight where every one of the records of current task will be found. Simply go to the up left corner as well as open the 'Untitled (Workplace)'. At the point when snap on, everything documents will show up as dropdown menu. To discover the content manager to alter the 'Code', select 'src' and the open 'main.cpp'. The word processor mode will show up on the Home Screen with opening another Tab. Here you can compose all codes of Current Ongoing Project.

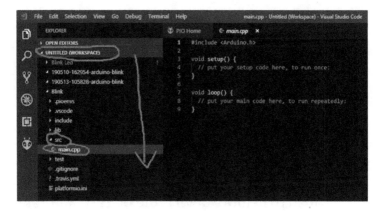

- Basically compose the Blink Code for Arduino UNO. Note that, the PlatformIO doesn't have the default access to Arduino libraries, so everytime you compose the code for Arduino, consistently incorporate Arduino library for example "#include <Arduino.h>" toward the start of program.

- The following stage would arrange and transferring the code. To do as such, how about we take a gander at the capacities given by the PlatformIO. Likewise the PlatformIO chooses the COM Port as a matter of course. Be that as it may, you can modify the Port in the event that it isn't the ideal COM port. The difference in COM port will be clarified later in this instructional exercise. PlatformIO has capacities like Build, Upload, Upload to Remote Device, Clean, Test, Run Task, Serial Monitor, New Terminal. Every one of the capacities can be found in the left base corner of the Editor. When you Hover over the symbols, the capacities will be appeared.

To Build the Sketch, click on 'Assemble' and to transfer the sketch click on the 'Transfer' Icon. At the point when the transfer is done, you will almost certainly observe the time taken to transfer with every other detail and a message saying "Achievement". The code is transferred effectively and you will most likely observe the Blinking of LED in the Arduino Board.

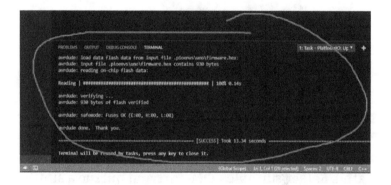

To choose or change any COM Port, simply go to the PlatformIO Home Screen and after that go to the Devices, here you can see all the accessible gadgets associated. Select suitable COM port and pursue a similar methodology to Upload the sketch.

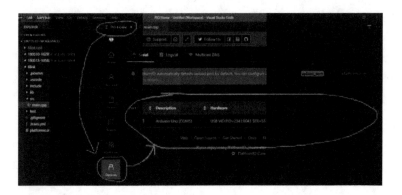

Programming STM32 Board using the PlatformIO IDE

Programming the STM32 Board will have precisely comparative advances like Programming Arduino UNO clarified previously. The distinction will choose the Board for STM32 when opening another undertaking for STM32. The beneficial thing about the PlatformIO is, it needn't bother with any outside bundle for any board to download independently, it consequently downloads every one of the bundles and makes it simple for us to choose a board and go to editorial manager. We will utilize outer JLink/ JTAG/STLink/Serial Programmer to transfer sketch to STM32. STM32 can likewise be modified with Arduino IDE. Continue with following strides to program it with PlatformIO.

- Simply name the Project (Here it is 'Flicker STM32'). At that point select the board for STM32 for example 'BluePill F103C8(Generic)'. At that point select Framework as Arduino. Snap on Finish and hang tight for quite a while as at first it will require some investment to download the bundles and conditions for board STM32.

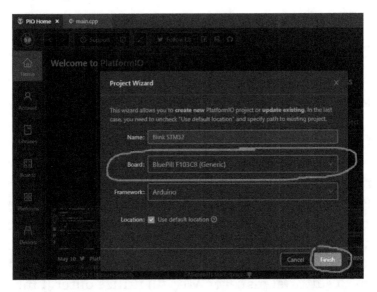

- When Set Up, the following task creation time will be less contrast with first. Presently Simply go to Untitled(Workspace) - > src - > main.cpp in the left document traveler.

- Presently the up and coming advances will be significant as it should be chosen what developer we should use for programming the STM32 Board. There are numerous software engineers accessible, for example, JTAG, STLink, JLink, Serial and so on. All will work yet you have to design the 'platformio.ini' setup page or document.

- In this Project, we are utilizing Serial Programmer CP210x USB to UART Bridge. We as of now have done Programming STM32F103C8 Board utilizing USB Port, o the vast majority of steps will be taken from that point as it were. You can visit the connection and discover progressively about this.

- Right off the bat, Connect Serial Programmer to STM32 Board with following pin mapping as well as interface it to PC.

USB to Serial Programmer	STM32 Board
5V	5V
Gnd	Gnd
Rx	A9
Tx	A10

- Presently go to the undertaking adventurer and open 'platformio.ini' page and change the announcement as appeared in the image. The upload_protocol will tell what software engineer should utilize (STLink, JLink, Serial and so on). The upload_port chooses the COM port. You can discover by going to 'Gadgets' in Home Page. Change the COM port as per your COM port.

Anbazhagan k

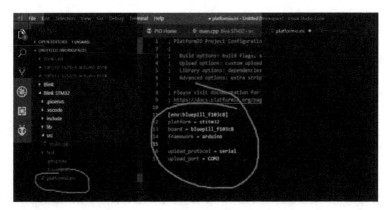

Go to the 'main.cpp' and change the program to Blink program. Presently simply transfer the program and it will indicate achievement message and time taken to transfer. Presently the LED will begin flickering associated at PC13 stick of STM32 board.

This completes the total instructional exercise on

programming the Arduino UNO just as STM32 Board utilizing PlatformIO. On the off chance that you have face any challenges while following the means, at that point please keep in touch with our gathering or remark underneath.

Code

```
#include <Arduino.h>
void setup() {
// initialize digital pin LED_BUILTIN as an output.
pinMode(LED_BUILTIN, OUTPUT);
}
// the loop function runs over and over again forever
void loop() {
digitalWrite(LED_BUILTIN, HIGH); // turn the LED on
(HIGH is the voltage level)
delay(100); // wait for a second
digitalWrite(LED_BUILTIN, LOW); // turn the LED off
by making the voltage LOW
delay(100); // wait for a second
}
```

◆ ◆ ◆

9.INTERFACING GT511C3 FINGER PRINT SENSOR (FPS) WITH ARDUINO

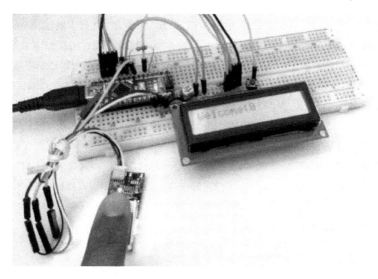

Biometrics has been utilized as a solid confirmation framework for quite a while now. Today there exist complex biometric frameworks which can recognize an individual by his heart beat mood or even by his DNA. Other doable strategies incorporate voice acknowledgment, Face acknowledgment, Iris examining and Finger print Scanning. Out of which the unique mark acknowledgment is the most broadly utilized technique, we can discover it from a basic participation framework to advanced mobile phones to Security checks and substantially more.

In this instructional exercise we will figure out how

to utilize the mainstream GT511C3 Finger Print Sensor (FPS) with Arduino. There are numerous FPS accessible and we have as of now figured out how to utilize them to assemble structures like Attendance framework, Voting Machine, Security framework as well as so on. However, the GT511C3 is further developed with high exactness and quicker reaction time, so we will figure out how to utilize it with Arduino to enlist fingerprints on it and after that distinguish the fingerprints at whatever point required. So how about we begin.

Materials Required

1. Bread board
2. GT511C3 Finger Print Sensor
3. Arduino Nano/UNO
4. Pot – 10k as well as 1k,10k,22k resistors
5. 16x2 LCD screen
6. Connecting Wires
7. Push button

GT511C3 Fingerprint Sensor (FPS) Module

Before plunging into the venture let us comprehend about the GT511C3 unique finger impression sensor Module and how it functions. This sensor is altogether different structure the Capacitive and Ultrasonic Fingerprint sensor that are regularly utilized in our advanced cells. The GT511C3 is an optical Fingerprint sensor, which means it depends on pictures of your unique mark to perceive its example. Indeed you read that right, the sensor really has a camera inside it which takes photos of your uncommon finger impression and after that procedures these pictures utilizing amazing in-constructed ARM Cortex M3 IC. The beneath picture demonstrates the front and rear of the sensor with pinouts.

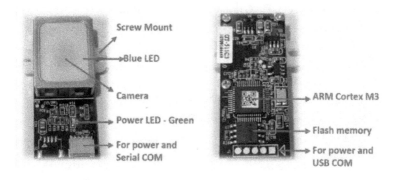

As should be obvious the sensor has a camera (dark spot) encompassed by blue LEDs, these LEDs must be lit up to take a reasonable picture of the uncommon finger impression. These pictures are then prepared and changed over into parallel an incentive by utilizing the ARM Microcontroller combined with EEPROM. The module likewise has a green shading SMD LED to show control. Each unique mark picture is of 202x258 pixels with a goals of 450dpi. The sensor can enlist upto 200 fingerprints and for each unique mark layout it relegates an ID structure 0 to 199. At that point during identification it can consequently contrast the examined unique mark and each of the 200 formats and if a match is discovered it gives the

ID number of that specific finger impression utilizing the Smack Finger 3.0 Algorithm on the ARM Microcontroller. The sensor can work from 3.3V to 6V and imparts through Serial correspondence at 9600. The correspondence pins (Rx and Tx) is said to be just 3.3V tolerant, anyway the datasheet does not indicate much about it. The stick out of a GT511C3 FPS is demonstrated as follows.

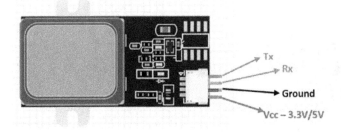

Aside from sequential correspondence the module can likewise be legitimately interfaced to PC however USB association utilizing the pins appeared in past picture. When associated with PC the module can be controlled utilizing the SDK_DEMO.exe application which can be downloaded from the connection. This application enables the client to select/check/erase fingerprints and furthermore to perceive fingerprints. The product can likewise assist you with reading the picture caught by the sensor which merits trying it out. Then again you can likewise utilize this Software regardless of whether the sensor is associated with Arduino, we will talk about on this later in this article.

Another fascinating component about the sensor is the metal packaging around detecting locale. As I advised before the blue LED must be turned on for the sensor to work. Be that as it may, in applications where the sensor ought to effectively sit tight for a unique finger impression it is beyond the realm of imagination to expect to keep the LED turned on consistently since it will warmth up the sensor and hence harm it. Subsequently in those cases the metal packaging can be wired to a capacitive touch info stick of a MCU to recognize in case that it is being contacted. In case that yes the LED can be turned on and the detecting procedure can be begun. This technique isn't exhibited here for what it's worth outside the extent of this article.

When working at 3.3V the sensor devours about 130mA. It requires almost 3 seconds for selecting a finger and 1 second to distinguish it. Be that as it may if the selected layout tally is less the acknowledgment speed will be high. For more insights regarding the sensor you can allude to this datasheet from ADH-Tech who is the official producer of the module.

Connecting GT511C3 Finger Print Sensor with Arduino

The GT511C3 FPS has two power pins which can be fueled by +5V stick of Arduino and two correspondence pins Rx and Tx which can be associated with any advanced stick of Arduino for sequential correspondence. Moreover we have likewise included a push catch and a LCD to show the sensor status. The total circuit chart for interfacing GT511C3 FPS with Arduino can be found beneath.

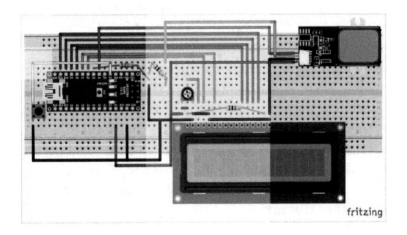

Since the Rx and Tx pins are 3.3V tolerant we have utilized a potential divider on the Rx side to change over 5V to 3.3V. The 10k resistor and 22k resistor changes over the 5V signal from the Arduino Tx stick to 3.3V before it arrives at the Rx stick of the FPS. The Sensor can likewise be controlled by 3.3V however ensure your Arduino can source enough current for the sensor. We have associated the LCD in 4-piece mode fueled by 5V stick of Arduino. A push catch is associated with stick D2 which when squeezed will place the program in enlist mode where the client can select new finger. In the wake of selecting the program will stay in filtering mode to examine for any finger contacting the sensor.

Arduino with GT511C3

As referenced before the GT511C3 FPS conveys through sequential correspondence, the sensor comprehends hex code and for each hex code a specific activity is performed. You can check the datasheet to realize all the hex qualities and its comparing capacity in case you are intrigued. However, fortunate for us bboyho has just made a library which can be utilized straightforwardly with Arduino to Enroll and identify fingerprints. The Github library for GT511C3 FPS can be downloaded from the connection beneath

GT511C3 Arduino Library

The connection will download a ZIP document, you would then need to add it to your Arduino IDE by following the order Sketch - > Include Library - > Add .ZIP Library. When you have included the library restart your IDE and you ought to have the option to discover the model projects for GT511C3 FSP under File - > Example - > Fingerprint Scanner TTL as demonstrated as follows

You should see four model projects, the flicker program will squint the blue drove on the FPS, the select and ID finger program can be utilized to enlist and recognize the fingers likewise. Note that a finger once selected will consistently be recollected by the module regardless of whether it is fueled off.

The Serial Pass-through program can be transferred to the Arduino to utilize the Demo_SDK.exe application that we examined before in this article. To erase any unique mark layout or to spare a duplicate on your PC this SDK application can be utilized.

Programming Arduino for GT511C3 Finger Print Sensor

Our point here is to compose a program that will select a finger when a catch is squeezed and show the ID number of the finger that is now enlisted. We must have the option to show all data on the LCD to empower the undertaking to be an independent one. The total code to do the equivalent is give at the base of this page. Here I am breaking the equivalent into little pieces to enable you to see better.

As consistently we start the program by including the required libraries, here we will require the FPS_GT511C3 library for our FPS module, Software sequential to utilize D4 and D5 on sequential correspondence and Liquid precious stone for LCD interfacing. At that point we have to make reference to which sticks the FPS and LCD is associated with. On the off chance that you had pursued the circuit graph all things considered, at that point it is 4 and 5 for FPS and D6 to D11 for LCD. The code for the equivalent is demonstrated as follows

```
#include "FPS_GT511C3.h" //Get library from https://github.com/sparkfun/Finger-print_Scanner-TTL

#include "SoftwareSerial.h" //Software serial library

#include <LiquidCrystal.h> //Library for LCD

FPS_GT511C3 fps(4, 5); //FPS connected to D4 and D5

const int rs = 6, en = 7, d4 = 8, d5 = 9, d6 = 10, d7 = 11; //Mention the pin number for LCD connection

LiquidCrystal lcd(rs, en, d4, d5, d6, d7); //Initialize LCD method
```

The direction fps.SetLED(true) will turn on the blue LED on the sensor, you can turn it off by fps.SetLED(false) when not required as it would warmth up the sensor whenever left on persistently. We have like-wise made the stick D2 as information stick and associated it to inward dismantle up resistor in order to interface a push catch to the stick.

```
void setup()

{

  Serial.begin(9600);

  lcd.begin(16, 2); //Initialise 16*2 LCD

  lcd.print("GT511C3 FPS"); //Intro Message line 1

  lcd.setCursor(0, 1);

  lcd.print("with Arduino"); //Intro Message line 2

  delay(2000);

  lcd.clear();

  fps.Open();       //send serial command to initialize fp

  fps.SetLED(true);   //turn on LED so fps can see fingerprint

  pinMode(2,INPUT_PULLUP); //Connect to internal pull up resistor as input pin
```

```
}
```

Inside the void circle work we need to check if the catch is squeezed, whenever squeezed we will enlist another finger and spare its layout with an ID number by utilizing the select capacity. If not we will continue trusting that a finger will be squeezed in the sensor. Whenever squeezed we will indentify the unique mark by contrasting it with all selected fingerprints format utilizing the 1:N technique. When the ID number is found we will show welcome pursued by the ID number. In case the unique finger impression did not coordinate with any of the selected fingers the id tally will be 200, all things considered we will show welcome obscure.

```
if (digitalRead(2))//If button pressed

{

Enroll(); //Enroll a fingerprint

}
// Identify fingerprint test

if (fps.IsPressFinger())

{
```

```
fps.CaptureFinger(false);

int id = fps.Identify1_N();

  lcd.clear();

  lcd.print("Welcome:");

  if (id==200) lcd.print("Unkown "); //If not rec-
ognised

  lcd.print(id);

  delay(1000);

}
```

The enlist capacity would need to take three example contributions to select one finger effectively.
Once enlisted a format for that specific finger will be
made which won't be erased except if the client constrained it however HEX directions. The code to select a finger is demonstrated as follows. The strategy
IsPressFinger is utilized to check in the event that a
finger is identified, in case that indeed, at that point
the picture is caught utilizing CaptureFinger and
after that at last Enroll1, Enroll2 and Enroll3 is utilized for three distinct examples to effectively enlist
one finger. The LCD shows the ID number of the finger
whenever selected effectively else it would show a

disappointment message with code. Code 1 methods the unique finger impression was not caught unmistakably and thus you need to attempt once more. Code 2 is a memory bomb sign and code 3 is to demonstrate that the finger has just been enlisted.

```
void Enroll() //Enrol function from library ex-
maple program

{

  int enrollid = 0;

  bool usedid = true;

  while (usedid == true)

  {

    usedid = fps.CheckEnrolled(enrollid);

    if (usedid==true) enrollid++;

  }

  fps.EnrollStart(enrollid);

  // enroll
```

```
lcd.print("Enroll #");

lcd.print(enrollid);

while(fps.IsPressFinger() == false) delay(100);

bool bret = fps.CaptureFinger(true);

int iret = 0;

if (bret != false)

{

  lcd.clear();

  lcd.print("Remove finger");

  fps.Enroll1();

  while(fps.IsPressFinger() == true) delay(100);

  lcd.clear(); lcd.print("Press again");

  while(fps.IsPressFinger() == false) delay(100);

  bret = fps.CaptureFinger(true);

  if (bret != false)
```

```
{
    lcd.clear(); lcd.print("Remove finger");

    fps.Enroll2();

    while(fps.IsPressFinger() == true) delay(100);

    lcd.clear(); lcd.print("Press yet again");

    while(fps.IsPressFinger() == false) delay(100);

    bret = fps.CaptureFinger(true);

    if (bret != false)
    {
        lcd.clear(); lcd.print("Remove finger");

        iret = fps.Enroll3();

        if (iret == 0)
        {
            lcd.clear(); lcd.print("Enrolling Success");
        }
    }
```

```
    else

    {

      lcd.clear();

      lcd.print("Enroll Failed:");

      lcd.print(iret);

    }

  }

    else lcd.print("Failed 1");

  }

  else lcd.print("Failed 2");

}

  else lcd.print("Failed 3");

}
```

Working of GT511C3 Finger Print Sensor with Arduino

Since our equipment and code is prepared the time has come to test our venture. Transfer the code to Arduino and power it up, I am simply utilizing the smaller scale usb port to control the venture. On booting we should see the introduction message on the LCD and after that it should show "Hi!..". This implies FPS is prepared to filter for finger, if any selected finger is squeezed it would state "Welcome" trailed by the ID number of that finger as demonstrated as follows.

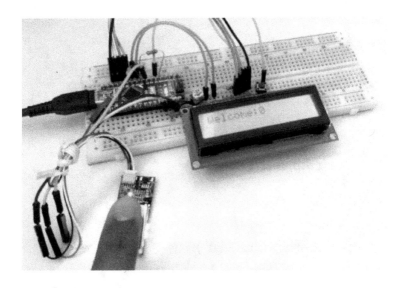

In case that another finger must be selected, at that point we can utilize the push catch to get into enlist mode and adhere to the LCD guidance to enlist a finger. After the selecting procedure is finished the LCD will show "Hi!.." again to demonstrate that it is perused to indentify fingers once more.

From here you can create many intriguing stuff on top on this utilizing the Finger Print sensor module. Expectation you comprehended the instructional exercise and delighted in structure something valuable, in case you have any inquiries leave them in the remark segment or utilize the gatherings for other specialized inquiries.

Code

```
/*
* Arduino with GT511C2 FingerPrint Sensor (FPS)
* Code to enroll and Detect Fingers
* Connect Tx of FPS to Arduino Pin D4 and Rx of FPS to D5
*/
```

```
#include "FPS_GT511C3.h" //Get library from https://
github.com/sparkfun/Fingerprint_Scanner-TTL
#include "SoftwareSerial.h" //Software serial library
#include <LiquidCrystal.h> //Library for LCD
FPS_GT511C3 fps(4, 5); //FPS connected to D4 and D5
const int rs = 6, en = 7, d4 = 8, d5 = 9, d6 = 10, d7 = 11; //
Mention the pin number for LCD connection
LiquidCrystal lcd(rs, en, d4, d5, d6, d7);//Initialize
LCD method
void setup()
{
 Serial.begin(9600);
 lcd.begin(16, 2); //Initialise 16*2 LCD
 lcd.print("GT511C3 FPS"); //Intro Message line 1
 lcd.setCursor(0, 1);
 lcd.print("with Arduino"); //Intro Message line 2
 delay(2000);
 lcd.clear();
  fps.Open();       //send serial command to initialize
fps
 fps.SetLED(true);  //turn on LED so fps can see finger-
print
  pinMode(2,INPUT_PULLUP); //Connect to internal
pull up resistor as input pin
}
void loop()
{
 if(digitalRead(2)==0)//If button pressed
 {
 Enroll(); //Enroll a fingerprint
```

```
}
// Identify fingerprint test
 if (fps.IsPressFinger())
 {
  fps.CaptureFinger(false);
  int id = fps.Identify1_N();
   lcd.clear();
   lcd.print("Welcome:");
    if (id==200) lcd.print("Unkown "); //If not recog-
nised
   lcd.print(id);
   delay(1000);
 }
 else
 {
    lcd.clear(); lcd.print("Hi!....."); //Display hi when
ready to scan
 }
}
void Enroll() //Enrol function from library exmaple
program
{
 int enrollid = 0;
 bool usedid = true;
 while (usedid == true)
 {
  usedid = fps.CheckEnrolled(enrollid);
  if (usedid==true) enrollid++;
 }
 fps.EnrollStart(enrollid);
```

```
 // enroll
lcd.clear();
lcd.print("Enroll #");
lcd.print(enrollid);
while(fps.IsPressFinger() == false) delay(100);
bool bret = fps.CaptureFinger(true);
int iret = 0;
if(bret != false)
{
 lcd.clear();
 lcd.print("Remove finger");
 fps.Enroll1();
 while(fps.IsPressFinger() == true) delay(100);
 lcd.clear(); lcd.print("Press again");
 while(fps.IsPressFinger() == false) delay(100);
 bret = fps.CaptureFinger(true);
 if(bret != false)
 {
  lcd.clear(); lcd.print("Remove finger");
  fps.Enroll2();
  while(fps.IsPressFinger() == true) delay(100);
  lcd.clear(); lcd.print("Press yet again");
  while(fps.IsPressFinger() == false) delay(100);
  bret = fps.CaptureFinger(true);
  if(bret != false)
  {
   lcd.clear(); lcd.print("Remove finger");
   iret = fps.Enroll3();
   if(iret == 0)
   {
    lcd.clear(); lcd.print("Enrolling Success");
```

```
  }
  else
  {
   lcd.clear();
   lcd.print("Enroll Failed:");
   lcd.print(iret);
  }
 }
  else lcd.print("Failed 1");
 }
 else lcd.print("Failed 2");
 }
 else lcd.print("Failed 3");
}
```

10.ARDUINO MULTITASKING TUTORIAL - HOW TO USE MILLIS() IN ARDUINO CODE

Arduino Multi-Tasking

T he performing multiple tasks has driven the PCs to a transformation where at least one projects can run at the same time which builds effectiveness, adaptability, flexibility and profitability. In installed frameworks, microcontrollers can likewise deal with Multitasking and performs at least two assignments all the while without ending the present guidelines.

Here in this instructional exercise we will figure out How Arduino performs Multitasking. For most part a postponement() work is utilized in Arduino for an intermittent assignment like LED Blinking yet this deferral() work end the program for some complete time and don't enable different activities to perform. So this article clarifies how we can maintain a strategic distance from utilization of postponement() work and supplant it with millis() to perform more than one errands all the while and make the Arduino a Multitasking controller. Before broadly expounding we should begin with downplaying Multitasking.

What is Multitasking?

Performing multiple tasks just means executing more than one undertaking or program at the same time simultaneously. Practically all working frameworks include performing multiple tasks. This sort of working frameworks are known as MOS (performing multiple tasks working framework). The MOS can be versatile or work area PC Operating System. The genuine case of performing multiple tasks in PCs are when clients run the email application, web program, media player, games, simultaneously and if clients don't need utilize the application it keeps running out of sight if not shut. The end client utilize every applications simultaneously however OS takes this idea somewhat extraordinary. How about we talk about how OS oversees performing multiple tasks.

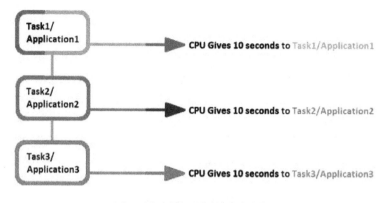

(a) Multitasking in Computers

As found in the image, the CPU isolates the time in the three equivalent parts and dole out each part to each assignment/application. This is the means by which the performing multiple tasks is done in a large portion of the frameworks. The idea will be practically same for the Arduino Multitasking, aside from the time dispersion will be somewhat extraordinary. Since the Arduino keeps running in low recurrence and RAM contrast with Laptop/Mobile/PC so the time given to each assignment will likewise be unique. Arduino likewise has a deferral() work which is utilized generally. Yet, before beginning we should talk about that why we ought not utilize delay() work in any undertaking.

Why to skip delay() in Arduino?

In the event that the reference documentation of Arduino is considered, at that point there is two sort of defer capacities, the first is postponement() and second is delayMicroseconds(). The two capacities are indistinguishable regarding creating delay. The main distinction, in deferral() work, the parameter whole number passed is in milliseconds i.e on the off chance that we compose delay(1000) at that point the postpone will be of 1000 milliseconds for example 1 second. Likewise in delayMicroseconds() work, the parameter passed is in microseconds for example in the event that we compose delayMicroseconds(1000), at that point the postpone will be of 1000 microseconds for example 1 milliseconds.

Here comes the point, the two capacities stop the program for the measure of time go in postpone work. So on the off chance that we are giving a deferral of 1 second, at that point the processor can't go to next guidance until 1 second passed. Additionally in case the deferral is 10 seconds, at that point program will stop for 10 seconds and processor won't permit to go for the following directions until the 10 seconds passed. This hampers the exhibition of the microcontroller as far as speed and executing the directions.

The best guide to clarify the downside of defer capacity is utilizing two push catches. Consider we need to flip two LEDs utilizing two push catches. So on the off chance that one push catch is pushed, at that point the relating LED should sparkle for 2 seconds, correspondingly in the event that second is pushed, at that point LED should gleam for 4 seconds. However, when we use delay(), on the off chance that the client is squeezing the principal catch, at that point the program will stop for 2 seconds and on the off chance that the client presses the second catch before 2 seconds delay, at that point the microcontroller won't acknowledge the contribution as the program is in end organize.

The official documentation of Arduino unmistakably makes reference to this in its Notes and Warnings of postponement() work depiction. You can experience and look at this to make it all the more clear.

Why to use millis() ?

To beat the issue brought about by utilizing delay, a designer should utilize millis() work which is anything but difficult to utilize once you become routine and it will utilize 100% CPU execution immediately in executing the guidelines. millis() is a capacity that just restores the measure of milliseconds that have passed from the Arduino board started running the present program without solidifying the program. This time number will flood (i.e return to 0), after roughly 50 days.

The same as Arduino have delayMicroseconds(), it additionally has the small scale adaptation of millis() as micros(). The distinction among micros and millis is that, the micros() will flood after around 70 minutes, contrasted with millis() which is 50 days. So relying on the application you can utilize millis() or micros().

Using millis() instead of delay():

To utilize the millis() for timing and deferral, you have to record and store the time at which the move made spot to begin the time and after that check at interims whether the characterized time has passed. So as expressed, store the present time in a variable.

---

unsigned long currentMillis = millis();

We need two additional factors to see if the required time has passed. We have put away the present time in currentMillis variable yet we additionally need to realize that when did the planning time frame begin and to what extent is the period. So the Interval as well as previousMillis is pronounced. The interim will reveal to us the time deferral and previosMillis will store the last time the occasion has happened.

---

unsigned long previousMillis;

unsigned long period = 1000;

To get this current, how about we take a case of a basic flickering LED. The period = 1000 will disclose to us that the LED will squint for 1 second or 1000ms.

```
const int ledPin =  4; // the LED pin number con-
nected

int ledState = LOW;      // used to set the LED state

unsigned long previousMillis = 0; //will store last
time LED was blinked

const long period = 1000;      // period at which to
blink in ms

void setup() {

  pinMode(ledPin, OUTPUT); // set ledpin as out-
put

}

void loop() {

unsigned long currentMillis = millis(); // store the
current time

  if (currentMillis - previousMillis >= period) { //
check if 1000ms passed

  previousMillis = currentMillis;  // save the last
```

```
time you blinked the LED

  if (ledState == LOW) { // if the LED is off turn it
on and vice-versa

    ledState = HIGH;

  } else {

ledState = LOW;

}

  digitalWrite(ledPin, ledState);//set LED with
ledState to blink again

  }

}
```

Here, the announcement <if (currentMillis - previousMillis >= period)> checks if the 1000ms has passed. In the event that 1000ms has passed, at that point the LED flicker and again comes to same state. Furthermore, this goes on. That is it, we have figured out how to utilize millis rather than postponement. Along these lines it won't end the program for specific interim.

Hinders in Arduino works same as in different microcontrollers. The Arduino UNO board has two separate pins for connecting hinders on GPIO stick 2 and 3. We have canvassed it in detail in Arduino Interrupts Tutorial, where you can get familiar with Interrupts and how to utilize them.

Here we will demonstrate Arduino Multitasking by taking care of two errands simultaneously. The undertakings will incorporate flickering of two LEDs in various time delay alongside a push catch which will be utilized to control the ON/OFF territory of LED. So three undertakings will be performed all the while.

Components Required

1. Three LEDs(Any Color)
2. Arduino UNO
3. Jumpers
4. Resistances (470, 10k)
5. Breadboard

Circuit Diagram

The circuit outline for exhibiting Arduino Multitasking is exceptionally simple and doesn't have much segments to connect as demonstrated as follows.

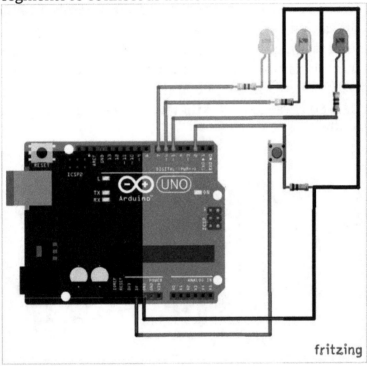

Programming Arduino UNO for Multitasking

Programming Arduino UNO for performing various tasks will just require the rationale behind how millis() work which is clarified previously. It is prescribed to practice squint LED utilizing millis over and over to make the rationale obvious and make yourself OK with millis() before beginning to program Arduino UNO for performing multiple tasks. In this instructional exercise the hinder is additionally utilized with millis() all the while for performing various tasks. The catch will be an interfere. So at whatever point a hinder is created for example push catch is squeezed, the LED will change to ON or OFF state.

The programming begins with proclaiming pin numbers where LEDs and Push Button are associated.

```
int led1 = 6;

int led2 = 7;

int toggleLed = 5;

int pushButton = 2;
```

Next we compose a variable to store the status of LEDs for sometime later.

```
int ledState1 = LOW;

int ledState2 = LOW;
```

Similarly as clarified above in the squint model, the factors for period and previousmillis is pronounced to look at and produce delay for LEDs. The primary LED squints at after each 1 second and another LED flickers at after 200ms.

```
unsigned long previousMillis1 = 0;

const long period1 = 1000;

unsigned long previousMillis2 = 0;

const long period2 = 200;
```

Another millis capacity will be utilized to produce the debounce deferral to keep away from the various presses of push catch. There will be comparative methodology as above.

```
int debouncePeriod = 20;

int debounceMillis = 0;
```

The three factors will be utilized to store the status of push catch as interfere with, switch LED and push catch state.

```
bool buttonPushed = false;

int ledChange = LOW;

int lastState = HIGH;
```

Characterize the activity of stick what stick will fill in as INPUT or OUTPUT.

```
pinMode(led1, OUTPUT);

  pinMode(led2, OUTPUT);

  pinMode(toggleLed, OUTPUT);

  pinMode(pushButton, INPUT);
```

Presently characterize the interfere with stick by joining hinder with meaning of ISR and intrude on Mode. Note that it is prescribed to utilize digitalPinToInterrupt(pin_number) when pronouncing attachInterrupt() capacity to decipher the real advanced stick to the particular intrude on number.

```
attachInterrupt(digitalPinToInterrupt(pushButton), pushButton_ISR, CHANGE);
```

The interfere with subroutine is composed and it will just change the buttonPushed banner. Note that, intrude on subroutine ought to be as short as could reasonably be expected, so attempt to compose it and limit the additional guidelines.

```
void pushButton_ISR()

{

  buttonPushed = true;

}
```

Circle begins with putting away the millis esteem in a currentMillis variable which will store the estimation of time slipped by each time the circle repeats.

```
unsigned long currentMillis = millis();
```

There is in complete three capacities in performing various tasks, flicker one LED at 1 second, Blink second LED at 200ms and If push catch is squeezed then turn OFF/ON LED. So we will compose three sections to do this errand.

The first is switches LED state after each 1 second by contrasting the millis slipped by.

```
if (currentMillis - previousMillis1 >= period1) {

  previousMillis1 = currentMillis;

  if (ledState1 == LOW) {

    ledState1 = HIGH;

  } else {

    ledState1 = LOW;

  }

  digitalWrite(led1, ledState1);

}
```

Likewise the also it flips the LED after each 200ms by looking at the passed millis. The clarification is as of now clarified before in this article.

```
if (currentMillis - previousMillis2 >= period2) {

  previousMillis2 = currentMillis;

  if (ledState2 == LOW) {
```

```
    ledState2 = HIGH;

  } else {

  ledState2 = LOW;

  }

  digitalWrite(led2, ledState2);

}
```

In conclusion, the buttonPushed banner is checked and in the wake of producing a debounce deferral of 20ms it just flips the territory of LED relates to push catch joined as intrude.

```
if (buttonPushed = true)  // check if ISR is called

{

  if ((currentMillis - debounceMillis) > debounce-
Period && buttonPushed)  // generate 20ms de-
bounce delay to avoid multiple presses

  {

    debounceMillis = currentMillis;      // save the
last debounce delay time
```

```
    if (digitalRead(pushButton) == LOW && last-
State == HIGH)    // change the led after push but-
ton is pressed

  {

    ledChange = ! ledChange;

    digitalWrite(toggleLed, ledChange);

    lastState = LOW;

  }

    else if (digitalRead(pushButton) == HIGH &&
lastState == LOW)

  {

    lastState = HIGH;

  }

    buttonPushed = false;

  }

}
```

This completes the Arduino millis?() Tutorial. Note

that so as to get ongoing with millis(), simply practice to execute this rationale in some different applications. You can likewise extend it to utilize engines, servo engines, sensor and different peripherals.

Complete code can be found beneath.

Code

```
/* Arduino Multitasking
*/
int led1 = 6;   // led1 connected at pin 6
int led2 = 7;   // led1 connected at pin 7
int toggleLed = 5;  // push button controlled led connected at pin 5
int pushButton = 2;  // push butoon connected at pin 2 which is also interrupt pin
int ledState1 = LOW; // to determine the states of led1 and led2
int ledState2 = LOW;
unsigned long previousMillis1 = 0; //store last time LED1 was blinked
const long period1 = 1000;   // period at which led1 blinks in ms
unsigned long previousMillis2 = 0; //store last time LED2 was blinked
const long period2 = 200;     // period at which led1 blinks in ms
int debouncePeriod = 20;      // debounce delay of 20ms
int debounceMillis = 0;       // similar to previousMil-
```

```
lis
bool buttonPushed = false;   // interrupt routine but-
ton status
int ledChange = LOW;   // to track the led status last
int lastState = HIGH;   // to track last button state
void setup() {
 pinMode(led1, OUTPUT);         // define pins as input
or output
 pinMode(led2, OUTPUT);
 pinMode(toggleLed, OUTPUT);
 pinMode(pushButton, INPUT);
    attachInterrupt(digitalPinToInterrupt(pushBut-
ton), pushButton_ISR, CHANGE);   // use interrupt
pin2
}
void pushButton_ISR()
{
 buttonPushed = true; // ISR should be as short as pos-
sible
}
void loop() {
  unsigned long currentMillis = millis(); // store the
current time
  if (currentMillis - previousMillis1 >= period1) {   //
check if 1000ms passed
    previousMillis1 = currentMillis;   // save the last
time you blinked the LED
   if (ledState1 == LOW) { // if the LED is off turn it on
and vice-versa
    ledState1 = HIGH;  //change led state for next iter-
```

ation

```
 } else {
  ledState1 = LOW;
 }
  digitalWrite(led1, ledState1);   //set LED with led-
State to blink again
 }
 if (currentMillis - previousMillis2 >= period2) { //
check if 1000ms passed
   previousMillis2 = currentMillis;   // save the last
time you blinked the LED
  if (ledState2 == LOW) { // if the LED is off turn it on
and vice-versa
   ledState2 = HIGH;
 } else {
  ledState2 = LOW;
 }
   digitalWrite(led2, ledState2);//set LED with led-
State to blink again
 }
 if(buttonPushed = true)  // check if ISR is called
 {
    if ((currentMillis - debounceMillis) > deboun-
cePeriod && buttonPushed)  // generate 20ms de-
bounce delay to avoid multiple presses
  {
   debounceMillis = currentMillis;    // save the last
debounce delay time
   if (digitalRead(pushButton) == LOW && lastState
== HIGH)    // change the led after push button is
```

```
pressed
  {
   ledChange = ! ledChange;
   digitalWrite(toggleLed, ledChange);
   lastState = LOW;
  }
   else if (digitalRead(pushButton) == HIGH && last-
State == LOW)
  {
   lastState = HIGH;
  }
  buttonPushed = false;
 }
 }
}
```